U-47 IN SCAPA FLOW

The Sinking of HMS *Royal Oak* 1939

ANGUS KONSTAM

First published in Great Britain in 2015 by Osprey Publishing,

PO Box 883, Oxford, OX1 9PL, UK

PO Box 3985, New York, NY 10185-3985, USA

E-mail: info@ospreypublishing.com

Osprey Publishing, part of Bloomsbury Publishing Plc

A CIP catalogue record for this book is available from the British Library

Print ISBN: 978 1 4728 0890 5

PDF ebook ISBN: 978 1 472 80891 2

ePub ebook ISBN: 978 1 4728 0892 9

Index by Fionbar Lyons

Typeset in Sabon

Maps by bounford.com

3D BEVs by Alan Gilliland

Originated by PDQ Media, Bungay, UK

Printed in China through Worldprint Ltd

15 16 17 18 19   10 9 8 7 6 5 4 3 2 1

Osprey Publishing supports the Woodland Trust, the UK's leading woodland conservation charity. Between 2014 and 2018 our donations are being spent on their Centenary Woods project in the UK.

www.ospreypublishing.com

DEDICATION

This book is dedicated to Agnes E. Ratter (née Millar) of Kirkwall, and to the remaining members of the Royal Oak Survivors' Association. Together they have safeguarded the memory of those who lost their lives on HMS *Royal Oak*. Also to the members of the Royal Naval Association (Orkney), the Royal British Legion (Kirkwall), and to the people of Orkney. Each year they ensure that the sacrifice of these young sailors will never be forgotten.

ACKNOWLEDGEMENTS

My special thanks to Kinlay Francis, of Orkney Uncovered. He operates a superb history-themed tour service in Orkney, and his knowledge of and insight into the events described here have been of great value to me. It is also important to mention the helpful staff of the Orkney Library & Archive. They maintain a valuable archive of material relating to Prien's raid, and the sinking of *Royal Oak*.

CONTENTS

INTRODUCTION

Scapa Flow. It's a place that conjures up conflicting images. In two world wars it was the Royal Navy's main anchorage during the naval campaigns against Germany. It became synonymous with British naval might – something that is now a distant memory. To many who served there Scapa was a miserable place, far from the comforts of home, where there was little to break the monotony in that vast and remote anchorage. Others saw the charm of Scapa Flow, which can be a beautiful, magical place, particularly during the long summer nights. To Orcadians it is simply 'The Flow', the virtually landlocked expanse of water which has become steeped in history. Orcadians are also well aware that beneath its surface lie the remains of 833 men and boys whose lives were snatched away three-quarters of a century ago, when the battleship they served in became their grave.

That battleship was HMS *Royal Oak*, a veteran of Jutland, and a floating home to almost 1,000 British sailors. On the night of 13–14 October 1939 these men and boys thought they were safe, as their battleship was securely anchored inside Scapa Flow. Instead, death was stalking them in the shape of a German U-boat, *U-47*, which had breached the defences of Scapa Flow, and was on the loose inside the anchorage, her commander searching for a suitable target for his torpedoes. He found it in *Royal Oak*, whose crew were oblivious to the threat. Shortly after 1am on 14 October the battleship was struck by a salvo of torpedoes, and sank within minutes. Many of her crew had no chance to escape – hence the high death toll. Every year, on 14 October, their loss is remembered, and a dignified low-key service is held over the wreck site. Ironically, the crew of *U-47* also lie entombed on the seabed of the North Atlantic, although the exact location of the craft is unknown.

The bare bones of the story are reasonably straightforward. On the evening of 13 October 1939 *U-47*, commanded by Günther Prien, entered Scapa Flow by way of Kirk Sound, a narrow channel that was supposedly sealed by a line of sunken blockships. Prien threaded his way past these obstructions, and reached the vast anchorage that lay beyond them. At first he headed west, towards the main fleet anchorage, but found it was deserted. So, he altered course to the north, towards the upper end of Scapa Flow. There he came upon *Royal Oak*, lying at anchor just under a mile from the north-eastern shore of Scapa Flow. Prien fired three torpedoes, but only one of them hit his target. Even so it was a glancing blow, as it struck her anchor cable. He then turned his boat around and fired his stern tube. That missed too.

Prien and his men were surprised that their attack hadn't led to the alarm being raised, but as Prien's men reloaded their bow tubes *Royal Oak* remained placidly at anchor. When the tubes were ready he fired again, and this time there was no reprieve for the battleship. *Royal Oak* was hit by up to three torpedoes, and began listing heavily as water poured into her hull. She slowly rolled over and sank, before most of her crew could scramble out onto the upper deck and throw themselves into the water. A few thousand metres to the south *U-47* turned away, and headed back to Kirk Sound. She left Scapa Flow the way she had come in, passing the blockships again to reach the open sea. By dawn *U-47* was off the Moray Firth, where she spent the day lying submerged to avoid detection. Travelling at night and lying submerged by day, the boat re-crossed the North Sea to Kiel. On 17 October the crew of *U-47* reached Kiel, where they were welcomed as heroes.

As the commander of *U-47*, *Kapitänleutnant* Günther Prien (1908–41) had already conducted one war patrol in the boat before he was selected to lead 'Special Operation P'. His high degree of professionalism made him the ideal candidate for the mission.

Günther Prien's raid on Scapa Flow was probably the most celebrated submarine attack of World War II, a feat of seamanship and daring that humbled the Royal Navy, and caused a significant blow to its naval power in North European waters. The Germans certainly regarded it as a triumph, as Prien had successfully broken into the anchorage the defences of which had proved too tough for German submariners during the previous war. It was a propaganda victory of considerable proportions during those opening months of the war, and Prien became a national hero. On the British side the Admiralty was forced to recognise that Scapa Flow was far from impregnable, and the key ships of the fleet were sent elsewhere until the great anchorage could be made secure.

Unfortunately, while this basic outline of Prien's raid on Scapa Flow is generally regarded as fact, being supported by the testimony of German and British sailors alike, the details of the enterprise are a lot less straightforward. Here the accounts of *Royal Oak* survivors are often at odds with the claims made by Prien and his men, and the official German version of what happened before and after the attack has been contradicted by other German accounts. To add to the problem, the ghostwritten autobiography of Günther Prien embellished the story of the raid, which muddied the waters even more. For instance, these various versions of the story disagree about the visibility that night, the number of British warships in Scapa Flow and even the number of warships that were torpedoed. These discrepancies have confounded more than a few historians over the years, which has only added to the general confusion.

Untangling these accounts has been difficult, but ultimately it has been a rewarding exercise. A comparison of original British and German documents and the testimony of those who were there has helped to build up a picture of what happened. This has been bolstered by the evidence provided by Scapa Flow itself, in the form of the wreck of the battleship, the discovery of torpedo fragments and a modern survey of the seabed. The result is an account of Prien's raid on Scapa Flow which is probably as close as we can get to the events that October night more than three-quarters of a century ago.

HMS *Royal Oak* pictured while on fleet gunnery exercises, shortly before the outbreak of World War II. Although changes in battleship design had largely rendered her unfit for front-line service, her powerful armament of eight 15in guns ensured she remained a useful asset.

SCAPA FLOW IN THE GREAT WAR

The Great War U-boat menace

The idea that a U-boat could break into Scapa Flow and wreak havoc was first mooted at the outbreak of World War I. On 3 August 1914 Admiral Sir John Jellicoe raised his flag on HMS *Iron Duke*, becoming the new commander of the Grand Fleet. The bulk of his ships were gathered in Scapa Flow, an anchorage the Royal Navy had used several times during the previous decade. The following morning the fleet put to sea, and as war was declared it was conducting a sweep of the North Sea. Scapa Flow, though, would remain its wartime base – the place it returned to after each operation. While Scapa was a wonderful natural harbour, and an ideal wartime anchorage for the Grand Fleet, it was not without its drawbacks. Orkney lay 525 miles north of the Admiralty in London, telegraph facilities were limited, and land communications involved a ferry crossing and a 24-hour rail journey on what became known as the 'Jellicoe Express'.

Worst of all, the anchorage was virtually undefended. At first, a few guns were landed to form makeshift shore batteries, and warships guarded the entrances to Scapa Flow. The Admiralty deemed the anchorage beyond the reach of enemy U-boats. This notion lasted less than a week. On 9 August the light cruiser *Birmingham* spotted a U-boat steaming on the surface, just a few dozen miles north of Orkney. *U-15* was rammed and sunk before she could submerge. This demonstrated that Scapa Flow lay well within range of German submarines. All a U-boat commander needed was a dark night, luck with the tides and a steady nerve. The fleet did what it could – fishing nets were used as makeshift anti-submarine nets, and were strung across the two main entrances to Scapa Flow at Hoy Sound and Hoxa Sound, while the larger warships of the Grand Fleet deployed their own anti-torpedo nets.

The stern of a Type VIIb U-boat, pictured in 1939 as she manoeuvres astern towards a quayside. Eight boats of this class were in service at the outbreak of war, including *U-47*. These craft had a better fuel capacity and torpedo tube configuration than their predecessors.

15 JANUARY 1914

HMS *Royal Oak* is laid down

This fear of U-boats manifested itself in the bizarre 'First Battle of Scapa Flow'. It started on the evening of 1 September, when a periscope was supposedly spotted in the water. Throughout the night destroyer searchlights probed Scapa Flow and shots were fired at suspicious objects, but no U-boat was found. Taking no chances Jellicoe ordered the battleship squadrons to put to sea. While this proved a false alarm – one of several that summer – it highlighted the vulnerability of the anchorage to U-boat attack. In a letter to Winston Churchill, First Lord of the Admiralty, Jellicoe wrote, 'I long for a submarine defence at Scapa. It would give such a feeling of confidence. I cannot sleep half as well inside as outside, mainly because I feel we are risking such a mass of vulnerable ships, in a place where, if a submarine did get in, she practically had the whole British fleet at her mercy ...'

While it would take time to replace these makeshift submarine nets with proper ones, the Admiralty was able to seal the smaller entrances into Scapa Flow. Between September 1914 and October 1915 a total of 23 old merchant ships were sunk in these channels. Of these, 15 were scuttled before the end of the year. A total of five ships were sunk in Burra Sound, blocking a smaller channel which merged with Hoy Sound, the western entrance to Scapa Flow. The remainder was sunk between the string of islands on the eastern side of Scapa Flow – Lamb Holm, Glims Holm, Burray and South Ronaldsay. One of these channels was Kirk Sound, which separated the small uninhabited island of Lamb Holm from the Orkney mainland. Here a total of four blockships were sunk in the channel, three during the winter of 1914–15, and the fourth the following September. It was an effective solution to the problem. These blockships, combined with the strong current through these channels, meant that these smaller entrances were now secure.

The disquiet felt by Jellicoe wasn't helped by several U-boat sightings around Orkney, real or imagined. On 16 October one was reported inside Scapa Flow itself – a report that prompted another hasty departure by the Grand Fleet, and the 'Second Battle of Scapa Flow'. As Churchill put it, 'Guns were fired, destroyers thrashed the waters, and the whole gigantic armada steamed out to sea in haste.' Later seals were blamed for the sighting.

Then, on the morning of 23 November 1914, a real German U-boat appeared at the entrance to Scapa Flow. She was *U-18*, commanded by *Kapitänleutnant* (Lieutenant) von Hennig – one of a number of U-boats operating off Orkney at the time. The previous evening von Hennig saw searchlights shining in Scapa Flow, which suggested the Grand Fleet was at anchor there. He decided to attempt to penetrate the anchorage's defences, and attack a dreadnought.

23 NOVEMBER 1914

***U-18* becomes the first U-boat to attempt to enter Scapa Flow**

HMS *Royal Oak*, manoeuvring at speed during an exercise off the coast of Orkney, June 1939. During the inter-war years her secondary guns were upgraded, giving her an effective anti-aircraft battery. So, when in Scapa Flow she was usually anchored within range of the radar station at Netherbutton, so that she could protect the installation from air attack.

A Type VIIb U-boat under way in the North Sea. As well as the 8.8cm deck gun shown here, these boats carried 14 torpedoes and were fitted with four bow tubes (with two reloads) and one stern tube (with a single reload).

U-18 had spent the night submerged in the Pentland Firth, but early in the morning of 23 November von Hennig took his boat into Hoxa Sound, the main entrance to Scapa Flow. He used his periscope to look into the anchorage. He saw no sign of the main fleet, and spotting an anti-submarine net ahead of him he decided to withdraw. At 11.20am his periscope was seen and the alarm was raised. Von Hennig stayed submerged, hoping to avoid detection. Then he collided with a minesweeper, which wrecked the periscope and damaged the steering gear. Without his periscope von Hennig was effectively blind. The U-boat hit a rock 50m below the surface of Hoxa Sound, the boat's buoyancy tanks were damaged, and the U-boat was forced to the surface. There she was promptly rammed by another guard ship, close to the entrance to the Pentland Firth, but the boat limped away before running aground on the jagged rocks of the Pentland Skerries.

Von Hennig scuttled *U-18* just as a British destroyer arrived, and he and 25 of his men were taken prisoner. Amazingly, only one German seaman was killed during the attack. Amusingly, an Orcadian lookout on South Ronaldsay reported seeing a cluster of men standing on the deck of a U-boat. When the report was telephoned through to naval headquarters the lookout was told he clearly didn't know the difference between a U-boat and a whale. The lookout retorted, 'Well, if it's a whale it's got 25 men standing on its back.' The following day – 24 November – two more U-boats – *U-16* and *U-22* – made a similar attempt to enter Hoxa Sound. *U-16* saw the Grand Fleet wasn't at anchor and withdrew without being detected, while *U-22* developed engine trouble, and was forced to abandon the attempt. So, more by luck than judgement the first U-boat attack on Scapa Flow ended in failure.

The Admiralty decided to keep the news of *U-18's* sinking a secret. This was to encourage the Germans to think that the U-boat had been sunk while trying to penetrate the anchorage's defences – perhaps in a minefield, or being caught in torpedo nets. The last thing they wanted the Germans to know was that the U-boat attack had only been thwarted by accident. Meanwhile the Admiralty worked hard to fortify its base. By December 1914 the first of three booms had been strung across the remaining entrances to Scapa Flow – Hoxa Sound, Switha Sound and Bring Deeps, the inner portion of the Hoy Sound entrance. While these were designed to stop destroyer attacks, by the summer of 1915 purpose-built steel anti-submarine nets had been strung across the same channels, replacing the makeshift fishing nets, and lookout and searchlight stations had been established around the shores of these channels.

By the middle of 1915 'induction loops' had been strung across the entrances to Hoxa Sound and Hoy Sound. These were magnetically charged cables which lay in loops on the seabed, and were designed to detect the magnetic fluctuation caused by a U-boat attempting to breach Scapa Flow's defences. This served as an early warning device, buying time for patrol vessels to intercept the U-boat. Further inside the entrances was a 'guard loop' – a second induction cable which was there to confirm the reading from the outer loop. Further on inside Hoxa Sound and Hoy Sound lay controlled minefields, which would be switched on by an operator on shore when ordered. The U-boat would then find itself in the middle of an active minefield.

These defences, combined with shore batteries and airship patrols, helped to render Scapa Flow a secure anchorage. For the rest of the war the Grand Fleet rode quietly at anchor there, when it wasn't out conducting sweeps into the North Sea, or countering sorties by the German High Seas Fleet. The Germans must have been convinced that the defences were formidable, as no other attempt was made to penetrate Scapa Flow until the closing weeks of the war. Instead the U-boats concentrated on minelaying off the Orkney coast. One such operation by *U-75* led to the sinking of the armoured cruiser *Hampshire*, which struck a mine off the west coast of Orkney on the evening of 5 June 1916, less than a week after the battle of Jutland. All but 12 of her 655-man crew were lost when *Hampshire* sank, as was Britain's Minister of War, Lord Kitchener, who was travelling to Russia on board the cruiser.

By late October 1918 the Allied naval blockade was causing mass hardship in Germany, the army was in retreat on the Western Front, and the Imperial German Navy was riven by mutiny. However, on 25 October approval was given to launch one last U-boat attack on Scapa Flow. *UB-116* set sail from Helgoland, under the command of *Oberleutnant zur See* (Sub Lieutenant) Hans Joachim Emsmann, with orders to penetrate the defences of Hoxa Sound. It was thought that as the Royal Navy used this entrance regularly, then it couldn't be mined. This was a fatal miscalculation. At 8.21pm on 28 October a hydrophone operator heard the sound of submarine engines. The induction loop also detected a U-boat, but then the contact was lost. At 11.30pm a periscope was sighted in Hoxa Sound itself, close to the line of the boom defences and the anti-torpedo net. For the last time in the war a U-boat was poised to enter Scapa Flow.

At that point the needle on the gauge linked to the guard loop quivered, indicating the U-boat was passing over the inner line of induction cables. The order was given to activate Hoxa Sound's controlled minefield. In fact, rather than let the U-boat strike a mine, the whole minefield was detonated. *UB-116* was torn apart in the explosion, and Emsmann and his 36 crew were killed instantly. All that remained of the U-boat was a mangled hull on the seabed. Two weeks later the war came to an end. Throughout the long conflict not one German warship had managed to breach the defences of Scapa Flow. The closest the Germans came was in late November, when the High Seas Fleet entered Scapa Flow following its surrender. There the ships

The business end of a Type VII U-boat – her four bow torpedo tubes, arranged one above the other on either side of the centreline. The torpedoes were loaded into the tubes by means of a system of chains and pulleys.

remained until the following summer, when they were scuttled by their own crews, as a last defiant gesture to avoid the fleet falling into Allied hands.

For almost everyone who had served in the Imperial German Navy, Scapa Flow was regarded with some degree of loathing. Not only had its defences proved inviolate, and it had served as the wartime base of their opponents, it was also a place that was now inextricably linked to the surrender of the High Seas Fleet. Many officers who had seen wartime service in the Imperial German Navy went on to serve in the Reichsmarine, the rump of the fleet that survived the war, and formed the navy of the German Weimar Republic. For them, Scapa Flow retained a 'bogeyman' quality, and was a name they associated with the victory of British seapower, and the shameful defeat of their own navy. It is little wonder that by 1935, when the Reichsmarine became the Kriegsmarine of Nazi Germany, some of these same officers harboured a dream to reclaim a little of their lost national pride. Ultimately, this would be done by launching an attack on the much-vaunted bastion of British naval power that was Scapa Flow.

ORIGINS

The calm before the storm

When World War I ended Scapa Flow ceased to be a hub of naval activity, tens of thousands of servicemen returned home, and the Grand Fleet was sacrificed on the altar of global disarmament. The British dreadnought fleet was scrapped in accordance with the terms of the Washington Naval Treaty (1922), with the exception of the handful of more modern battleships fitted with 15in guns, and a few battlecruisers. These included the battleships of the Royal Sovereign class, one of which was *Royal Oak*. Jellicoe's flagship *Iron Duke* also survived the disbanding of the dreadnought fleet, although

HMS *Royal Oak* was a Royal Sovereign-class battleship, which first saw service in May 1916, at the Battle of Jutland. The curve of her starboard anti-torpedo bulge can be clearly seen in this photograph of her, taken in September 1939.

she was relegated to second line duties, and eventually became a floating headquarters. In Orkney coastal batteries and booms were dismantled, minefields were cleared, and induction cables were recovered. Soon all that was left of Scapa Flow's wartime defences were the empty casements of gun batteries and searchlights, where sheep now found shelter, and the rusting blockships screening the anchorage's narrower entrances.

During the inter-war period the islands settled back into their old rhythm of life, although the war had wrought changes – communications had improved, electricity had arrived and technological improvements led to a boom in farming. In Scapa Flow itself, the salvage company Cox and Danks began raising the bulk of the scuttled German High Seas Fleet, a long and costly operation that tested the skills and ingenuity of the salvors, and the courage of the hard-hatted divers. Between 1924 and 1938 the company, and its successor Metal Industries Ltd, raised 38 German warships, including 11 capital ships. The battlecruiser *Derfflinger* was the last of them, but war broke out before she could be towed south to be scrapped. So, her upturned hull remained moored in Scapa Flow for the duration of World War II.

However, peace was relative – although Scapa's defences had been removed, stray mines continued to be washed up on beaches, or spotted by Orkney fishing boats. Wartime huts had long been sold off and transported to other parts of Orkney, to serve as farm buildings or outhouses, but otherwise the concrete remnants of gun emplacements and other defences still remained as a reminder of the war years. Strangely, from 1928 onwards, German cruise liners began to visit Orkney, and these tourists were able to see the enemy's great base for themselves – or what remained of it. They had come from a nation where unrest was becoming commonplace. The harsh terms of the Treaty of Versailles (1919) had created a feeling of injustice in Weimar Germany, as had the severe military crackdown on German revolutionaries in the immediate aftermath of the war.

Re-emergence of the U-boat threat

Over the next four years, amid political and social turmoil and aided by the brownshirted thugs of its SA paramilitary wing, Adolf Hitler's NSDAP or 'Nazi' party grew from a party with less than 3 per cent of the vote to the largest single party in the Reichstag. In 1933 Hitler was appointed Chancellor. Thereafter the slide to dictatorship was rapid. In Orkney the German cruise ships that visited between 1933 and 1937 now flew the marine jack of Germany – a flag bearing the Nazi swastika. The British began to recognise the threat posed by Nazi Germany from March 1935, following the abrogation of the Treaty of Versailles, and Germany's withdrawal from the League of Nations. This was followed by a large-scale militarization programme in Germany, one that involved the German Navy (the Reichsmarine) – a force that would become the Kriegsmarine before the end of the year.

Hitler had no desire to appear a threat to the Royal Navy before his fleet was stronger, so a diplomatic exchange led to the signing of the Anglo-German Naval Treaty of June 1935. At Versailles, Germany had been forbidden from

owning a U-boat fleet, as the Kaiser's U-boats had caused considerable damage to Allied shipping during the war. Having renounced the terms of the treaty Hitler was no longer bound by this. Now, thanks to the Anglo-German treaty, the Kriegsmarine could legitimately expand to a third of the size of the Royal Navy's surface fleet. Just as importantly, the Kriegsmarine now had British approval to build a small number of U-boats for use in German coastal waters. The Kriegsmarine, though, had no desire to limit the range and capability of its U-boats. In fact, plans were already drawn up for a new breed of ocean-going vessels, with the performance and capability to range far out into the Atlantic.

The development of this new U-boat fleet began slowly. In 1935–36 the first two experimental Type Ia U-boats were laid down, as well as six Type IIa coastal submarines (designated *U-1* to *U-6*). These were based on the export U-boats Germany had been building, as well as submarines already being used by Turkey, Spain and Finland – countries with similar ideologies to Nazi Germany. For years Germany had been building submarines in defiance of the Treaty of Versailles, and as a result of this 'export business' German shipyards had developed both the expertise and the technology needed to mass produce larger U-boats. Subsequent versions of Type II U-boats were launched between 1935 and 1940, but by then these craft were designated as being too small for the Kriegsmarine's wartime needs. What the navy required were boats that were true ocean-going craft.

So, in 1935 plans were approved for a new class of U-boat. The first design work on these vessels had begun two years earlier, and by the time the Anglo-German treaty was signed the plans were almost complete. The

HMS *Hood* pictured at anchor in Scapa Flow, framed by the guns of a battleship. The battlecruiser *Renown* – sister ship of *Repulse* – is on the far left of the photograph, taken in the main fleet anchorage off Flotta. None of these prestigious capital ships were in Scapa Flow when *U-47* carried out its raid.

MARCH 1933

Günther Prien becomes an officer cadet in the Reichsmarine

first of these boats was ordered in March 1935, and was launched the following June. By the end of 1936 nine of them had entered service. They were powerful weapons of war, with four bow tubes and one stern tube, as well as a deck gun. This first batch of ten boats was dubbed Type VIIa. The building of these new U-boats was only part of the project. The Kriegsmarine also needed crews for them, and so from March 1935 it began recruiting U-boat volunteers. These men were trained using the eight Type Ia and IIa boats, and a Naval Training School in Kiel was established to ensure the men were given a thorough grounding in the theoretical and practical aspects of their new profession.

As the first of these craft joined the fleet, plans for a slightly larger and more effective variant were approved, and orders were issued for their building. The first of these was laid down in November 1936, and production of these Type VIIb U-boats would continue until after the outbreak of war. While they appeared similar to the earlier batch, these boats had a larger fuel capacity, which gave the U-boats a greater range – up to 9,400 nautical miles. Interestingly, they were primarily designed to operate on the surface, where their twin diesel engines gave them a top speed of just under 18 knots. They were designed to submerge to make an attack, or to avoid trouble, but limited battery capacity and a slow speed of just 8 knots when submerged limited their underwater effectiveness. However, they were well armed, and designed to carry 14 torpedoes. This new generation of U-boats would be at the forefront of any naval campaign in the war that many were now seeing as inevitable. One of these new boats would be *U-47*.

By the spring of 1938 the first ocean-going Type VIIa and VIIb U-boats were ready to enter service, and crews were allocated to them after their training was complete. The professional training continued as the crews conducted dummy torpedo and gun attacks, or practiced evading detection,

HMS *Royal Oak*, pictured shortly after emerging from a major refit in 1934–36. An aircraft catapult was added to the top of 'X' turret, an experimental torpedo tube was fitted below 'A' turret, and her foremast and mainmasts were modified to support larger gunnery directors.

damage-control techniques and all sorts of other tasks aimed at honing their skills. The result was a growing number of powerful U-boats, with crews and commanders who were able to make the best possible use of their craft. Unfortunately for the Kriegsmarine, its planners assumed they would have several years to build up their U-boat fleet, and Germany wouldn't be involved in a major war before the summer of 1944. Instead, these new boats would be plunged into a new world war in the autumn of 1939.

In January 1936, the Kriegsmarine appointed *Kapitän zur See* Karl Dönitz as its *Führer der Unterseeboote* (Commander of Submarines). Dönitz, who became a Conteradmiral (Rear Admiral) in 1939, played a key role in planning the expansion of the *Ubootwaffe* (U-boat force), which he intended would number 300 ocean-going U-boats by 1944. Dönitz and his small staff were completely unprepared for Adolf Hitler's antagonism of Poland in the summer of 1939. East Prussia was a German enclave separated from the rest of Germany by 'the Polish corridor', and during the summer of 1939 Hitler laid the propaganda groundwork for an invasion. When this Blitzkrieg took place in September 1939 Great Britain and France honoured their pledge to support the Poles, and Europe was plunged into a new world war. Far from having 300 U-boats at his disposal, Dönitz now had to go to war with less than 60 vessels, many of which were Type II coastal boats.

In Britain, the Royal Navy was even less prepared for a war than the Kriegsmarine. Twelve of her ageing fleet of battleships and battlecruisers had seen service in World War I. The remaining three – the battlecruiser *Hood* and the battleships *Nelson* and *Rodney* – entered service during the 1920s, and improvements during the 1930s had been minimal. Although a new class of five battleships was laid down in 1937, these modern warships would not enter service for at least another year. The situation was a little better when it came to carriers, cruisers and destroyers, and new classes had entered service shortly before the outbreak of war, or were under construction. However, the fleet had global commitments, and so only a portion of these warships were earmarked for service in home waters. These would be based in Scapa Flow.

During the late 1930s the Admiralty realised that if a new war with Germany took place, Scapa Flow would be just as useful a base for the Home Fleet as it had been for the Grand Fleet during the previous war. In October 1937 Scapa was designated a 'Category A Defended Port'. While this sounded impressive, its defences were non-existent. That spring though, work began on the construction of oil storage tanks at Lyness on Hoy, designed to hold 100,000 tons of fuel oil for the fleet. The following year the first of these tanks became operational and booms were laid across the main entrances to Scapa Flow. In January 1939 the Admiralty declared that Scapa Flow would serve as its 'fleet base', and the pace of work increased. Anti-aircraft guns were dug in around the future fleet base at Lyness, while coastal batteries using 6in guns from the last war were established overlooking Hoy Sound and Hoxa Sound.

On board his flagship *Nelson*, the commander of the Home Fleet, Admiral Charles Forbes, felt he was slightly better placed than Jellicoe had

27 FEBRUARY 1937

U-47 is laid down

Captain William Benn (1889–1962), the commanding officer of HMS *Royal Oak*, was a highly experienced and well-respected figure, who had served in the Royal Navy for 35 years before assuming command of the battleship in July 1939.

been on *Iron Duke* a quarter of a century earlier. From 'A-Buoy' off Flotta a direct phone link connected him with the Admiralty in London, as well as the shore base at Lyness. *Iron Duke* herself had been pressed into service as the floating headquarters of Admiral Wilfred French, Admiral Commanding Orkney and Shetland (ACOS), who was in charge of the naval defences of the anchorage. New coastal guns appeared, and new anti-aircraft guns, while a radar station was established at Netherbutton, in Orkney's East Mainland. The Fleet Air Arm established a naval air station outside Kirkwall, while the RAF built two airfields across the Pentland Firth in Caithness. While these arrangements fell far short of providing peace of mind to Forbes and his sailors, the defences were being strengthened. It is unfortunate that international events moved faster than the pace of these improvements.

By August 1939 the main entrances to Scapa Flow through Hoxa Sound, Switha Sound and Hoy Sound were protected by booms and anti-submarine nets, rudimentary coastal batteries covered the same channels and basic air defences were in place. Combat air patrols and radar gave some degree of warning in the event of an air raid, and once again controlled minefields and induction loops were about to be laid across the main entrances to Scapa Flow. Army units arrived to protect the islands from invasion, and searchlight batteries began to dot the landscape. Plans were laid to protect the fleet from air attack using a combination of land-based anti-aircraft guns and the weapons of the ships themselves, creating a wall of flak to deter the Luftwaffe. By then, 44 ships of various types were anchored in Scapa Flow, including several capital ships – battleships, battlecruisers and aircraft carriers. It was hoped that by the end of the year the base would be deemed fully secure.

The weak point in these defences were the smaller entrances, particularly those on the eastern side of Scapa Flow. The blockships that protected these narrow channels during the previous war were no longer adequate. Winter storms had moved some of them, while others had been salvaged or cleared to allow local fishing boats to navigate their way through the channels. So, new ships were earmarked to be sunk, to seal off properly these four entrances – Kirk Sound, Skerry Sound, Weddell Sound and Water Sound. Only when this was done could the Home Fleet consider itself to be reasonably secure from attack. Until then, Admiral Forbes hoped the Germans hadn't noticed his Achilles' heel.

THE PLAN

Outbreak of war

At 11am on 3 September 1939, Great Britain declared war on Germany. Hitler had ignored the British demand to withdraw its troops from Poland – a British ally – and so the British cabinet had no option but to honour its treaty with the Poles. Word reached Admiral Forbes within minutes of the outbreak, but the Home Fleet was already on a war footing, and at sea. While Scapa Flow might still have lacked truly effective defences, the base was operational, and the warships themselves were ready for action. The most significant threat came from air attack, although the Home Fleet included the aircraft carrier *Ark Royal*, which could protect the fleet while it was at sea. Forbes could also enjoy air protection from the RAF when operating close to home, or when in Scapa Flow.

Forbes' two main tasks when the war began were to sweep the North Sea, the Norwegian Sea and the North Atlantic for German merchant ships, and to intercept German commerce raiders. The two *Panzerschiffe* (literally 'armoured ships', but better known as 'pocket battleships ') *Deutschland* and *Graf Spee* were already at sea, and had to be tracked down and sunk. He also had to prevent sorties by other German warships, the most notable being the battleships *Scharnhorst* and *Gneisenau* (erroneously referred to by the British as 'battlecruisers'), and a third *Panzerschiffe*, the *Admiral Scheer*. The Admiralty warned him that a battlecruiser, two pocket battleships and two cruisers were possibly in Icelandic waters, ready to begin commerce raiding in the Atlantic as soon as hostilities broke out. So, when the war began the battleships *Nelson* and *Rodney*, the older battleships *Royal Sovereign* and *Royal Oak*, the battlecruisers *Hood* and *Renown* and the carrier *Ark Royal* were already patrolling the area between Shetland and Norway. The sortie was uneventful, and the fleet returned to Scapa Flow on 6 September.

After that the Home Fleet settled down to something of a routine. Occasional sweeps were conducted, convoy movements were covered,

Karl Dönitz, pictured later in the war wearing the uniform of a *Viseadmiral* ('Vice Admiral'), after his promotion to the rank in September 1940. When 'Special Operation P' was planned, Dönitz was a *Kommodore* (Commodore), and the Kriegsmarine's *Führer der Unterseeboote* (Commander, U-boats).

3 SEPTEMBER 1939

Britain declares war on Germany

warships joined or were detached, and an unsuccessful attempt was made to draw out the German surface fleet. Twice, when the threat of air attack was deemed particularly high, the larger warships left Scapa Flow and took shelter in Loch Ewe, off the west coast of Scotland, which was deemed beyond the range of German bombers. The largest of these sweeps began on 8 October, when the battleship *Gneisenau* was sighted off the Norwegian coast. In fact this was merely a German attempt to lure the Home Fleet away from Scapa Flow, where it could be more easily attacked by the Luftwaffe. However, the Luftwaffe failed to make contact, and the Home Fleet returned empty-handed, with the bulk of its warships heading to Loch Ewe. By then, though, the Germans had already launched a fresh operation – a daring U-boat raid on Scapa Flow.

The first raid

In 1958, *Grossadmiral* (Grand Admiral) Dönitz published his memoirs. In them he described the thinking that lay behind the operation. In September 1939 Dönitz held the rank of *Kommodore* (Commodore) and commanded the *Ubootwaffe*. He wrote, 'The idea of taking action against Scapa Flow came to me at the beginning of the war. However, I first abandoned it because of the extraordinary technical difficulties, and also because of the memory of the two unfortunate attempts made during World War I by Lieutenant von Hennig and Sub Lieutenant Ensmann.' The technical difficulties he mentioned were the combination of strong currents in the area, and the likely presence of anti-submarine nets, minefields, blockships and patrol vessels. He reckoned that Admiral Forbes would have made sure that Scapa Flow's defences were secure before he used the anchorage as a base. In this respect he over-estimated the efficiency of the British war effort during those opening weeks.

Still, *Korvettenkäpitan* (Lieutenant Commander) Viktor Oehrn of the *Ubootwaffe* staff was more optimistic than his superior, and convinced Dönitz to consider the feasibility of a raid on the anchorage. Luftwaffe reconnaissance flights were requested, and *U-16* was dispatched to the Pentland Firth, to scout the Hoxa Sound entrance to Scapa Flow. *Oberleutnant zur See* Horst Wellner of *U-14* reported that entering Scapa Flow through the Hoxa channel would only be possible if the booms and nets were temporarily moved, to let British surface ships in or out of the anchorage. Dönitz received the first reconnaissance photographs on 26 September. They showed elements of the Home Fleet at anchor in the main fleet anchorage off Flotta, and revealed there were no anti-submarine nets in Scapa Flow, apart from the ones protecting the main entrances. Dönitz ruled out the possibility of penetrating the natural harbour through either Hoxa Sound or Hoy Sound. His attention was then drawn to the smaller channels on the eastern side of Scapa Flow:

In Holm Sound there are only two steamers which seem to be sunk across Kirk Sound, and another on the north side. To the south of the latter and up to Lamb Holm there are: a first gap 17 metres wide at [the] low water mark, where the depth reaches 7 metres, and a second, smaller [gap] to the north. On both sides the shore is almost uninhabited. I think it is possible to pass there during the night, and on the surface at flood tide. The greatest difficulty remains the navigation.

Kommodore Dönitz had spotted the Achilles' heel of Scapa Flow's defences. The steamers Dönitz referred to were the blockships that were sunk in Kirk Sound in 1914–15. The most northerly blockship was the steamer SS *Numidian*, which lay close to the northern shore of the channel, facing the Orkney mainland. To the south of her *Aorangi*, *Thames* and *Minieh* extended the barrier of wrecks to the shallows off the small uninhabited island of Lamb Holm. All of them had been heavily ballasted before they were scuttled and were expected to remain in place until they rusted to pieces. However, the smallest of them – *Minieh* – broke her back when she was scuttled, and was less of an obstacle than the others. After the war the

This Luftwaffe reconnaissance photograph taken on 2 October 1939 shows the two most northerly channels to the east of Scapa Flow – Kirk Sound (top) and Skerry Sound (bottom). In between them lies the island of Lamb Holm. In Kirk Sound, the three blockships marked (1) are *Soriano* (top) and *Thames* (bottom), while *Numidian* lies a little to the right (east) of *Soriano*. The areas marked (2) denote areas of shallow water and strong currents. This photograph was used by Dönitz and Prien during the planning of 'Special Operation P'.

Admiralty agreed to open the channel again to allow the fishermen of Holm village (or 'St Mary's) on the northern shore of Kirk Sound to reach the fishing grounds to the west of Orkney.

So, in 1920 *Aorangi* was raised by a Dundee salvage company, and was eventually deposited in the shallows off Cornquoy, a mile and a half to the east, and safely out of the way of local fishing boats. The ballast was also removed from *Numidian*, prior to her being moved too, but she was never raised. Instead the lightened blockship swung round to lie parallel to the shore, which effectively opened the channel to fishing boats without the need to move the vessel. *Minieh* fell apart altogether, and much of her hull was raised, but attempts to raise *Thames* were abandoned when it was discovered her hull was too fragile to lift. Instead her upper works were cut down and her stern removed, to reduce the obstruction she posed to fishermen. That left the remains of two blockships in place – the 4,836-ton passenger ship *Numidian* and the 1,327-ton packet steamer *Thames*.

Therefore in March 1939 the 2,642-ton American-built steamer *Soriano* (sometimes mistakenly referred to as *Seriano*) was sunk in the channel, just to the north of *Thames*. While the bows of *Thames* pointed southwards towards Lamb Holm, the bows of *Soriano* pointed towards the shore. These, together with the remains of *Numidian*, were the blockships Dönitz described in his memoirs. As he noticed from the aerial reconnaissance photograph, *Soriano* and *Thames* were only 40m apart, and this gap was likely to be sealed off by a boom of some kind. Two more promising gaps lay between the bows of *Soriano* and the shore of the Orkney mainland, 200m to the north, and the bows of *Thames* and the northern coast of Lamb Holm, 300m away to the south.

At high water Kirk Sound was around 600m wide. However, a Type VIIb U-boat on the surface had a draught of 4.75m, which reduced the width of the navigable channel by almost half. Then there were the blockships themselves. That left a U-boat with two options – passing close under the bows of *Soriano*, where the navigable gap was around 70m, or in front of *Thames*, where the navigable channel was 80m wide. Even then a U-boat with a 6.2m beam would have to pass as close as it could under the bows of one of the blockships at high tide, to avoid the risk of running aground in the shallows. A strong current flowed through Kirk Sound, which would make the passage even more dangerous, unless the attempt was made at slack water.

Unknown to Dönitz, Admiral French had ordered two additional obstacles to be put in place. The first was a thick rope hawser, linking the sterns of *Thames* and *Soriano*, from which lengths of anchor cable were hung, to snag any passing boat. Anchors and anchor cables were also laid across this 40m gap, to completely block the channel. Then, from the bows of *Soriano* a steel hawser was run out and attached to an anchor embedded on the northern foreshore of Kirk Sound. That left the channel to the south of *Thames*. A suitable ship – the 3,859-ton *Lake Neuchatel* – had been purchased, and was due to be sunk there by the third week of October. For the moment, though, the gap was still unplugged. Given the right conditions of tide and current, and with a bit of luck, a daring navigator could take a U-boat through Kirk Sound and enter Scapa Flow.

The man Kommodore Dönitz selected for this mission was *Kapitänleutnant* Günther Prien, the commander of the Type VIIb U-boat *U-47*. The 31-year-old U-boat commander was brought up far from the sea in Leipzig, but in 1923 became a cabin boy on the sailing ship *Hamburg*. Experience brought promotion with it, and in 1932 he was awarded his Master's certificate. However, the global recession meant he was unable to find work, and so in 1933 he became an Officer Cadet in the Reichsmarine. He opted for service in U-boats, and after promotion through the junior ranks he became a *Kapitänleutnant* in February 1939. Six weeks earlier, he was given his first command – *U-47*, which was commissioned in Kiel on 17 December 1938.

On 19 August, *U-47* left Kiel on her first patrol. By the time war was declared on 3 September she had reached her allotted hunting area in the Bay of Biscay. Prien claimed his first victim on 5 September. She was the 2,407-ton British steamer SS *Bosnia*, of the Cunard Steamship Company, heading home to Britain from Sicily with a cargo of sulphur, having learned of the declaration of war as she passed through the Straits of Gibraltar. At 9am that morning Prien surfaced 500m astern of her and fired shots with his 88mm deck gun. When the *Bosnia* radioed for help *U-47* fired in earnest. A shell hit the ship and started a fire in the cargo hold. *Bosnia*'s captain gave the order to abandon ship, and most of the crew took to the boats. They were soon picked up by the Norwegian tanker SS *Eidanger* – Norway being neutral at the time. However, one cadet had fallen overboard, and was picked up by the U-boat. Another officer was taken on board the U-boat for questioning, but both sailors were then released.

The following day *U-47* spotted another British ship – the 4,086-ton cargo steamer SS *Rio Claro*, owned by the Thompson Steamship Company. She had left Sunderland in the north-east of England before the outbreak of war, and was bound for Montevideo in Uruguay, carrying a cargo of coal. She was north-west of Cape Finisterre when *U-47* surfaced, and once again *U-47*'s gun crew went into action, after the steamer radioed for help, firing on her until the crew abandoned ship. The *Rio Claro* still refused to sink, so Prien finished her off with a single torpedo. She sank a few minutes later. The *Rio Claro*'s 41-man crew were all rescued by the Dutch cargo ship *Stad Maastricht*.

At 5pm on 7 September *U-47* came upon the smaller British steamer SS *Gartavon*, of 1,777 tons. She was 250 miles west-north-west of Cape Finisterre, when Prien's U-boat surfaced 500m off her port beam. The steamer belonged to the Gart Line, and was carrying a mixed cargo of iron ore, asphalt and other goods from La Goulette in Tunisia to Glasgow. Once again Prien was reluctant to waste his torpedoes, so he sank the *Gartavon* using his deck gun. All of her 25-man crew survived – after abandoning ship they were eventually rescued by the Swedish merchant vessel SS *Castor*. So, in the first week of the war *U-47* sank three British merchant ships, displacing a total of 8,270 tons. This was a successful operation by any standards.

Nowadays this string of islands on the eastern side of Scapa Flow is linked by the Churchill Barriers, but in 1939 the islands were separated by four channels, obstructed by blockships. In this photograph the mainland of Orkney is in the foreground, while beyond it lie the islands of Lamb Holm, Glimps Holm, Burray and South Ronaldsay. The channel in the foreground between the mainland and Lamb Holm is Kirk Sound, where Prien entered Scapa Flow. On the right of the photograph is the village of St Mary's, where Bobby Tullock's taxi headlight shone over the channel just as U-47 was passing through it. The line of blockships obstructing Kirk Sound is no longer visible, but the remains lie immediately to the right of No. 1 Churchill Barrier. (Charles Tait Photography)

However, hours after sinking the *Gartavon U-47* was recalled to Kiel – one of ten U-boats sent home in mid-patrol. Dönitz wanted to use these boats to attack targets in the North Atlantic, before the British could organize their shipping into convoys. However, he had a special mission in mind for Prien and *U-47*.

On both the outward and return voyages to the *U-47*'s patrol ground, Prien had sailed northwards around the top of the British Isles. The U-boat returned home to Kiel on 15 September, after 28 days at sea. The crew were delighted by their success, and by their unexpected return to base. However, Prien himself had little time to relax. On 1 October he was ordered to report to Dönitz's floating headquarters. He was joined by *Korvettenkapitän* Sobe, commanding Prien's 7th U-boat Flotilla, and newly promoted *Kapitänleutnant* Wellner of *U-14*, who had returned from patrol off Orkney just two days before. There Dönitz revealed his plan, codenamed 'Special Operation P'. Prien was to take *U-47* across the North Sea to Orkney. Once there he was to penetrate Kirk Sound, weaving his boat through the blockships, and so enter Scapa Flow. Once inside the anchorage, he was to cause the maximum damage possible, before escaping the way he had come in.

Midnight on 13/14 October was deemed the ideal time for the operation, in order to make passage through Kirk Sound at a suitably high tide and at slack water. *U-47* would set off on this special patrol on 8 October – in a week's time. Prien was given a few days to study the reports, charts and photographs, quiz Wellner, and decide whether or not he would accept the mission. Dönitz was under no illusion about the dangers. In his briefing he reminded Prien of the two failed attempts to penetrate Scapa Flow's defences during the previous war. He also stressed the navigational challenges Prien would face. That evening, Prien – a newlywed – had dinner with his wife

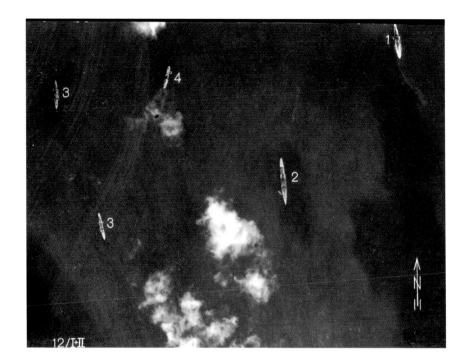

This aerial photograph of the Home Fleet at anchor was taken by a Luftwaffe reconnaissance aircraft on 2 October 1939. It shows *Royal Oak* (1) at anchor off Gaitnip, while the battlecruiser *Repulse* (2) lies at anchor to the south-west. A pair of light cruisers (3) and a supply ship (4) can also be seen in the image. It was probably this photograph which suggested to Prien that the battlecruiser was still anchored near *Royal Oak* on 13–14 October.

Ingeborg, then returned to the depot ship *Hamburg*, to pore over the documents. By morning he had decided to accept the task.

The following afternoon Prien requested another meeting with Dönitz and agreed to make the attempt. He then returned to *U-47* to supervise the preparation of his boat. This included the removal of her Type G7a torpedoes, which ran on compressed air, and the loading of 14 Type G7e torpedoes, which were electrically powered, and so showed no tell-tale stream of bubbles in their wake. Food, fuel, water and provisions were also taken on board, but only enough for a shorter than usual patrol – one lasting no more than two weeks. On 6 October, new reconnaissance photographs showed two capital ships in Scapa Flow – the battleship *Royal Oak* and the battlecruiser *Repulse*. Prien hoped they would still be there a week later.

On the evening of 6 October Prien invited his First Officer – *Oberleutnant zur See* Engelbert Endrass – to dinner on board the *Hamburg*, accompanied by the boat's senior NCO and navigator, *Obersteuermann* Wilhelm Spahr. In the privacy of his cabin Prien revealed their mission – a raid on Scapa Flow. The rest of the crew would be told of their destination after the boat had put to sea. Meanwhile, the three men had to remain silent about the mission – one that many would have seen as a near-suicidal enterprise.

5 SEPTEMBER 1939

U-47 sinks its first merchant ship of the war

THE RAID

Departure from Kiel

At 10am on Sunday 8 October 1939, *U-47* cast off from the Tirpitz mole in Kiel, and headed out into the Kieler Förde. No bands played, no crowds cheered – this was a deliberately low-key departure. From there the U-boat turned into the Kiel-Holtenau locks, which marked the entrance to the Kaiser Wilhelm Canal (now the Kiel Canal). The canal was 52 nautical miles long, and *U-47* completed its transit by 4pm. At Brunsbüttel the canal opened into the estuary of the River Elbe. Once out of the way of shipping Prien submerged the boat, and *U-47* lay on the bottom until midnight. Prien wanted to avoid detection by enemy aircraft or ships, and so during the voyage to Scapa Flow the boat would only steam on the surface under cover of darkness. During the day she would lie low on the seabed.

In the early hours of Monday 9 October Prien set a course of north by north-west, directly towards the German island of Helgoland. He spent the morning conducting diving tests, checking the trim of the boat and her ability to dive quickly and quietly. *U-47* spent the rest of the day lying off the harbour of Helgoland, before setting off again at nightfall. During the night she passed through Channel 1, a safe route through the defensive minefields that protected the German North Sea coast. By dawn they were approaching the Dogger Bank. Here Prien submerged again, to avoid detection by fishing boats, regardless of their nationality. The U-boat lay there until after nightfall on 10 October, when she surfaced again, started her main engines, and resumed her course towards the north-north-west, travelling at an easy 10 knots.

During this voyage the boat's log was particularly flavourless, as if the voyage was routine. For the 9th, Prien wrote, 'During day lay submerged – at night continued on course.' The entry for the following day read simply, 'As on previous day.' When the boat submerged at dawn on 11 October she lay approximately 90 nautical miles to the east of the Firth of Forth, and 170 nautical miles from her destination. The following evening Wilhelm Spahr checked his position and confirmed to Prien that *U-47* would reach the west coast of Orkney before dawn on Friday 13 October, despite the worsening weather. The voyage continued – the following day was spent lying on the seabed well to the east of Rattray Head, which is just north of the Scottish fishing port of Peterhead. During the night of 12–13 October *U-47* made good progress as she travelled past the Moray Firth, although the sea was rough and conditions uncomfortable. In fact a full gale had developed while they had been submerged, and as they steamed north the U-boat pitched and rolled throughout the night. Indeed, some of the crew were seasick. Finally, though, *U-47* passed the eastern entrance to the Pentland Firth at around 3am on the morning of 13 October.

Prien decided to continue on until he reached the latitude of Holm Sound, and then steam east for an hour, to place himself well clear of any warships passing in and out of Scapa Flow. So, shortly before dawn broke he submerged 15 nautical miles east of the sound. The U-boat would spend the day before its attack lying submerged, 80m below the surface of the North Sea. At least the weather was supposed to ease during the day, and Prien expected reasonably calm seas by the time he attempted his passage through Kirk Sound the following evening.

Kapitänleutnant Günther Prien (centre, in naval coat) surrounded by the crew of *U-47*, pictured in a commemorative photograph taken in Kiel in late October 1939. Due to the rotation of crews very few of these men were still on board *U-47* when she was sunk in the North Atlantic in March 1941.

The Home Fleet

The German U-boat crew weren't the only mariners to be caught in the gale. On Sunday 8 October, as *U-47* was transiting the Kaiser Wilhelm Canal, Admiral Forbes was on board his flagship *Nelson*, secured to 'A' Buoy in Scapa Flow. At 1.20pm he learned that the *Gneisenau* had been spotted, and two hours later the bulk of the Home Fleet put to sea, in an attempt to intercept the German battleship. Forbes divided his force into two groups. The battlecruisers *Hood* and *Repulse* sailed north towards the coast of northern Norway, accompanied by two light cruisers and four destroyers.

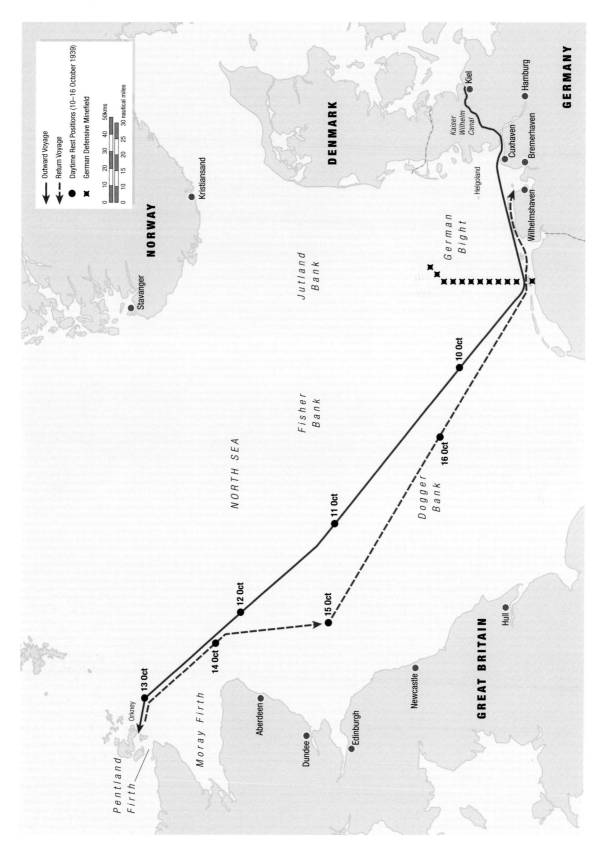

A few hours later *Nelson*, *Rodney*, the carrier *Furious*, a light cruiser and eight destroyers headed for a position north of Shetland. The two groups would then sail towards each other, hoping to catch the German battleship in a pincer. No contact was made, and at noon on 9 October the two groups rendezvoused halfway between Shetland and Norway.

Two more groups also took part in the hunt for the *Gneisenau*. The first was Humber Force, a group of cruisers and destroyers sent from Rosyth to patrol the Skagerrak. Then at 7.30pm on 9 October the battleship *Royal Oak* sailed from Scapa Flow escorted by two destroyers. She was too slow to keep up with the rest of the Home Fleet, so her job was to act as the 'backstop', guarding the passage between Orkney and Shetland in case *Gneisenau* slipped past the Home Fleet's 'pincers'. In fact, she and *Royal Sovereign* had spent part of the previous month patrolling the same area, in the week following the outbreak of war. The *Royal Sovereign* was now back in Plymouth, so if the *Gneisenau* did appear, *Royal Oak* would have to fight the German battleship on her own. However, all she encountered off Fair Isle was the gale Prien and his men would endure on their voyage north. It was worse off Fair Isle – cyclonic bad weather soon developed into a storm, Force 10 on the Beaufort scale.

The seas were violent enough to rip the battleship's Carley Float liferafts overboard and make life very uncomfortable for everyone on board. Of course, it was much worse for the crew of *Royal Oak*'s escorting destroyers, who were unable to keep station with the battleship. During the afternoon of 10 October *Royal Oak* lost contact with them and returned to Scapa Flow. She passed back through Hoxa Sound during the early hours of 11 October and was directed to anchor in the northern part of Scapa Flow, two miles from Scapa Pier, five cables off the eastern shore of the anchorage below Gaitnip. There her secondary batteries could help protect the radar station at Netherbutton, which lay half a mile inland, a little over 2,000 yards to the south-east of the battleship's anchorage. Scapa Flow's air defences were minimal, so in the event of an air attack these guns would be all-important, as the radar station was the key to Orkney's air defences.

The risk of air attack was certainly high. German aerial reconnaissance flights had flown over Scapa Flow several times over the past few weeks –

OPPOSITE
U-47's route across the North Sea, 8–17 October 1939.

8 OCTOBER

U-47 **leaves port, bound for Scapa Flow**

8 OCTOBER

Most of the Home Fleet leaves Scapa Flow in pursuit of *Gneisenau*

In this view of the *Royal Oak* wreck buoy, taken on the 75th anniversary of the sinking, the rugged coast below Gaitnip can be seen behind the Orkney Islands Council vessel *Flotta Lass*. Further to the left Scapa Pier can be seen, and behind it – a mile from the end of Scapa Bay – is the skyline of Kirkwall, dominated by the spire of St Magnus' Cathedral. The dead of *Royal Oak* are commemorated by a memorial there, which incorporates the ship's bell.

The ungainly HMS *Pegasus* was originally commissioned in 1914 as HMS *Ark Royal*, the world's first purpose-built seaplane carrier. She was renamed in 1934, and was used as a training vessel for seaplane crews and as an aircraft transport. On the night of 13–14 October she was anchored a little to the north of *Royal Oak*.

including the flights requested by Dönitz. The most recent had been on 12 September, as *U-47* was lying on the seabed off Aberdeenshire. In fact, the Luftwaffe had hoped the *Gneisenau* sortie would lure the Home Fleet out to sea, where it could more easily be attacked by bombers. No contact was made with Forbes' ships, but on 9 October Humber Force was bombed in the North Sea, with no ships being hit. A week later the same ships were attacked as they lay in the Firth of Forth. This time not only were no ships hit, but the RAF managed to intercept the returning bombers, shooting down several of them.

Forbes and the bulk of the Home Fleet remained at sea until the afternoon of 10 October, having continued the search for the *Gneisenau* despite the worsening weather. Then Forbes received a fresh report, saying that the German ships had returned to the Baltic. So, detaching *Repulse* and *Furious* to Scapa Flow to refuel, Forbes led the rest of the Home Fleet past Fair Isle and on towards Loch Ewe. He was concerned about Scapa Flow's lack of air defences after the attack on Humber Force. As a result *Furious*, *Hood*, *Nelson* and *Rodney* weren't in the anchorage when Prien penetrated Scapa Flow's defences. On the evening of 13–14 October they were 100 miles away, riding safely at anchor in Loch Ewe.

Still, when the Luftwaffe reconnaissance flight flew over Scapa Flow at 3pm on 12 October there were 63 Royal Naval vessels in the anchorage. The largest of these were the carrier *Furious*, the battlecruiser *Repulse* and the battleship *Royal Oak*. The old dreadnought *Iron Duke* was also there, a floating headquarters ship moored off Lyness. The other vessels consisted of six light cruisers, 13 destroyers, five minesweepers, nine armed merchant cruisers, a seaplane carrier, a store ship, a repair ship, a hospital ship, a netlayer and a cluster of tugs, boom defence drifters and armed patrol trawlers. A report of these sightings was radioed to Prien, but as he was submerged for most of 13 October he never received it.

In fact, two of the three most prestigious targets in Scapa Flow had already left the anchorage before Prien reached Orkney. *Repulse* left Scapa at 5.34pm on 12 October, bound for the dry dock in Rosyth. She was accompanied by two destroyers. Interestingly, she was heading south through the Moray Firth while *U-47* was on the last nocturnal leg of its journey to Orkney. U-boat and battlecruiser must have passed within 10 nautical miles of each other during the night. By 9am the following morning *Repulse* passed under the Forth Rail Bridge to enter Rosyth, after an uneventful passage. While *Repulse* was steaming south the carrier *Furious* slipped through Hoxa Sound, accompanied by two destroyers, and headed west through the Pentland Firth bound for Loch Ewe. That was an even more prestigious target which narrowly missed a high-seas encounter with Prien's U-boat.

While *U-47* lay submerged off the west coast of Orkney throughout 13 October other warships came and went from Scapa Flow. Three light cruisers left for their patrol stations off Iceland, one of them accompanied by three destroyers, while three light cruisers arrived in the anchorage, the last of them being the new cruiser *Belfast*, which anchored near 'A' buoy at 3.20pm. Finally another destroyer headed south for repairs in Rosyth. That meant that, on the night of 13–14 October, *Royal Oak* was the only capital ship in Scapa Flow. The light cruisers *Belfast*, *Caledon*, *Cardiff*, *Colombo* and *Delhi* were anchored in the main fleet anchorage north of Flotta, while the destroyers and auxiliary vessels were anchored off the coast of Hoy, between the island of Cava and Longhope Sound. Apart from the boom defence and patrol trawlers operating in Hoxa Sound and Hoy Sound, the only other warships in Scapa Flow by the evening of 13 October were *Royal Oak*, anchored off Netherbutton, and the seaplane carrier HMS *Pegasus*, anchored a mile to the north, midway between the battleship and Scapa Pier. In other words, all of the really important targets had left Scapa Flow before Prien arrived.

The venerable *Royal Oak* was no longer considered a front-line battleship. She had been in service for 23 years, and despite her powerful armament she was a warship from an earlier age. Launched in 1914, 'The Mighty Oak' was commissioned on 1 May 1916 and joined the Grand Fleet in time to take part in the battle of Jutland, fought just 30 days later. During her baptism of fire her eight 15in guns proved highly effective, and she scored three hits on the German battlecruiser *Derfflinger*. Ironically, the *Derfflinger* was now moored on the other side of Scapa Flow from *Royal Oak*, floating keel uppermost, waiting for the war to end so she could be cut up for scrap.

During the inter-war years *Royal Oak* underwent a few modifications, having anti-torpedo bulges added, and receiving extra anti-aircraft guns. The idea of the anti-torpedo bulge was that it extended below the waterline of the ship and out from the side, effectively creating a sacrificial ship's side. A torpedo striking this would detonate against it, and the water-filled void inside the bulk, rather than against the vitals of the ship itself. The problem was, this was not particularly effective, as torpedoes were now powerful enough to penetrate both layers. Also, the bulges slowed the ship down, which was why in 1939 *Royal Oak* could only make just over 20 knots, making her too slow to keep up with the more modern warships of the Home Fleet.

Still, *Royal Oak* remained useful. Her main armament of eight 15in guns was still potent, and if she had met *Gneisenau* off Fair Isle she would outgun the German battleship. Her fire control and gunnery direction systems had been improved as well, and her deck and belt armour increased. Other improvements included a new suite of 4in anti-aircraft guns, a pair of deck-mounted twin torpedo tubes and a seaplane, which was launched from a flying-off platform located on top of 'X' turret. For much of the inter-war period *Royal Oak* served in the Mediterranean. She was due to be sent back there, where her firepower would help counter the latent threat posed by the Italian fleet. Instead, war was declared before her redeployment, so she remained with the Home Fleet. Owing to her 'second line' status she was primarily used as an operational training ship for boy seamen, and as the anti-aircraft asset that saw her assigned a regular anchorage off Netherbutton.

A sizeable proportion of *Royal Oak's* crew were Boy Seamen – youngsters who were not old enough to serve in front-line ships, and who were still learning their trade. A total of 120 Boy Seamen served on the battleship and 48 of them were lost when she sank.

After arriving in Scapa Flow in the early hours of Wednesday 11 December and anchoring in her assigned position, the duty watches of *Royal Oak* spent the next two days repairing the damage caused by the storm, while her crew took turns to enjoy liberty in Kirkwall. The drifter *Daisy II* was assigned to her as her tender, and spent Thursday and Friday ferrying sailors between the battleship and Scapa Pier. From there Kirkwall was just a mile away, across the narrow isthmus between Scapa Bay and Kirkwall Bay. A 17-year-old local girl, Rita Spence (now Jamieson), lived on a farm near the pier that supplied milk to *Royal Oak*. That Friday afternoon she was chatting to one of the boy seaman – a lad her own age – and recalled him saying, 'We'll sleep well tonight – we're safe in Scapa Flow.' Neither of the teenagers knew he had less than ten hours to live.

Breaching Scapa Flow

Twenty-five miles to the south-east, *U-47* spent the day lying on the seabed, while her crew rested or ate their meals. During the voyage daytime and night-time routines had been reversed, so most of the crew tried to sleep, which saved oxygen. The members of the duty watch who remained at their stations wrapped cloths around their boots, to reduce noise. The boat's engineering officer *Oberleutnant* Hans Wessels supervised a small team which was busy repairing a fuel pipe. The last thing anyone wanted was a mechanical failure during the raid. Before the crew settled, Prien told them what their mission would be – the penetration of Scapa Flow's defences. Everyone knew the risks, and the fate of those who had attempted the same thing during the last war. Of course, most of them had guessed already – the limited food and fuel they embarked in Kiel would have told them this was

EARLY MORNING, 11 OCTOBER

Royal Oak returns to Scapa Flow

The blockships at the north side of Kirk Sound, photographed after the building of No. 1 Churchill Barrier. Before work began on the barrier, additional blockships were put in place to render the channel impassable. *Numidian* is in the foreground, with *Soriano* behind her. The *Thames* is on the far left of the photograph.

no ordinary mission. Then, a passing glance at the chart table would have told them where they were heading.

At 4pm the crew began to stir, and the boat's cook, an *Obergefreiter* (Leading Seaman), was already preparing the crew's meal – veal cutlets with green cabbage. It was served at 5pm. Prien spoke to Spahr the navigator, to check the boat's position, but both men knew this was only an estimate, as the currents and tides off Orkney were unpredictable. Spirits were high – Prien recorded in his log, 'The morale of the crew is excellent.' Shortly before 7pm the crew were called to their diving stations. 'Operation P' was about to reach its most dangerous phase. On Prien's order Wessels started the boat's electric motors, and the dive planes were tilted, allowing the boat to rise steadily at a controlled 1m per second. The ascent was paused to check and adjust the boat's trim, and then continued again until *U-47* was at periscope depth, the top of her conning tower about 5m below the surface of the North Sea. Once there Prien held the boat steady, and the periscope was raised. There were no enemy ships to be seen.

NIGHT OF 13/14 OCTOBER

U-47 enters Scapa Flow through Kirk Sound

While none of the blockships in Kirk Sound remain visible above water, these remains of the blockship SS *Lycia* in nearby Skerry Sound can still be seen, just east of No. 2 Churchill Barrier. After studying aerial photographs, Dönitz concluded that both Skerry Sound and Weddell Sound were impassable, so he recommended that Prien use the more northerly channel through Kirk Sound.

Noting which way the swell was running, Prien ordered the boat turned towards the south-east, putting the boat head on to the oncoming waves. Then he gave the order to surface. When the depth gauge read 10m the conning tower broke the surface, and Endrass opened the hatch. Within seconds he and Prien emerged onto the U-boat's tiny bridge, and began scanning the horizon. There was nothing to be seen. They were joined by the rest of the bridge watch, who shut the hatch behind them just as the periscope was being lowered. The diesel engines were started, the electric motors shut down and the boat got under way. Prien turned her towards the north-east, and *U-47* began moving towards the coast of Orkney, which lay ahead of them in the darkness. It was now approximately 7.15pm.

While the U-boat had lain on the seabed the weather had improved, and now the sea was relatively calm, apart from the north-westerly swell. The wind had also died down to a cold fresh breeze, coming from the north-north-east – the direction of the Arctic Sea. Their speed was increased to 17 knots, which by Spahr's calculation meant they would reach Holm Sound within the hour. Meanwhile, ventilation fans filled the boat with fresh air. As they moved inshore a stream of depth soundings reached the bridge from the control room, where Spahr was checking the chart. It was then that the bridge crew claim they first saw the lights in the sky – the flickering of the Aurora Borealis, or Northern Lights. This worried Prien slightly, as he preferred the sky to be as dark as possible. The period of the new moon had been chosen for exactly this reason. Still, he took solace in the fact that these light displays rarely lasted very long.

The same display was seen by others – to the east of Shetland the bridge crew of the British light cruiser *Sheffield* saw them, and recorded the sighting in the ship's log. A destroyer escorting the cruiser recorded the lights too, adding that they lasted for much of the watch (8pm until midnight). Others in Orkney saw them too, but there is no agreement about how long the display lasted. Then Prien saw something else. According to his memoirs he sighted a dark shape in the distance – the outline of another vessel. It was probably just a local fishing boat, but he decided to dive anyway, in case the U-boat was spotted and the alarm raised. *U-47* dived again, and once at periscope depth Prien took another look. There was no longer any sign of a vessel, but it was later claimed its propellers were heard. Either it had been imagined, or the craft had moved away. As no British warship was on patrol there, it was probably a neutral freighter.

The U-boat remained submerged for a while as it continued on towards the eastern coast of Orkney. Gradually the shape of the coast appeared and solidified. At 11.25pm the U-boat surfaced again. The Northern Lights had dimmed, yet the coast was identifiable. The U-boat lay to the east of South Ronaldsay, an island 8 miles long, and the most southerly of the chain of islands that lay between the North Sea and Scapa Flow. On its far side was Hoxa Sound, the well-guarded main entrance into Scapa Flow, while further to the south was the Pentland Firth, with its notorious eddies and currents. The bridge crew could make out Ward Hill, which at 118m was the highest point of the island. Looking to the north, Prien could make out the coast of the next island – Burray. That meant the entrance to Holm Sound and Kirk Sound lay approximately 5.5 nautical miles to the north.

It was later claimed that they could also see the lighthouse of Rose Ness, marking the northern edge of Holm Sound, but that is unlikely, as visibility was much less than 11,000 yards. A variation of this was the assertion that the lighthouses were switched on, but this was not corroborated by British records. They might have been lit earlier that evening, for the departure through Hoxa Sound of the light cruiser *Calypso*, but as the U-boat approached Holm Sound the lighthouse would have been in darkness. Following Spahr's recommendation the U-boat turned onto a new heading of 320 degrees. It would have taken *U-47* around 20 minutes to motor northwards, until she lay between Burray Ness – the easternmost tip of the island of Burray – and Rose Ness, on the south-east corner of the Orkney mainland. Between these two low headlands – 1.3 nautical miles apart – lay the entrance to Holm Sound.

Timing was critical. High water that night was 11.38pm, and it was now approximately ten minutes after that. This meant it was slack water – there was no appreciable tidal current running through Holm Sound, or the three smaller sounds that made up its western edge – Weddell Sound, Skerry Sound and Kirk Sound. There the tidal stream was all important, as these three channels were much narrower than the larger Sound. While Holm Sound divided Burray from the Orkney mainland, two small and uninhabited islands lay on the western side of the channel, separating it from Scapa Flow. These islands – Lamb Holm and Glimps Holm – were what divided Holm Sound into these three smaller channels. Prien's objective was the largest of these, and the most northerly – Kirk Sound – which ran between Lamb Holm and the mainland.

It took the U-boat another 15 minutes to move across Holm Sound and reach the entrance of Kirk Sound. To starboard lay the Orkney mainland – the parish of Holm, where the little church of St Nicholas stands near the shore, close to the farm of Cornquoy. The U-boat must have passed within a thousand yards of it as it headed through Holm Sound. The depth was shallowing fast. Spahr's chart told him that the water here was about 12m deep, but further into Kirk Sound it fell away to less than 8m in the centre of the channel. The draught of *U-47* was 4.7m, but Prien had ordered the ballast tanks to be filled slightly, to make the boat more stable during the passage through the sound. She now drew 5.1m, which meant there was little margin for error.

Spahr recommended a course change to 270 degrees, or due

Kapitänleutnant Günther Prien (centre), chatting to two Luftwaffe airmen rescued by *U-47* to the east of Orkney as the boat was on her way into the Atlantic on her sixth patrol. The airmen were returned safely to Kiel when *U-47* returned there in July 1940, after 34 days at sea.

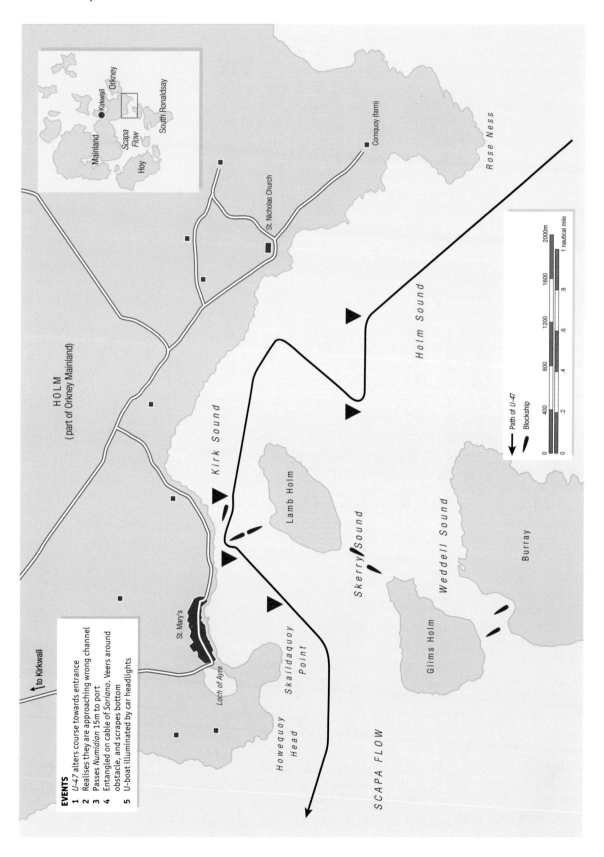

EVENTS

1 *U-47* alters course towards entrance
2 Realises they are approaching wrong channel
3 Passes *Numidian* 15m to port
4 Entangled on cable of *Soriano*. Veers around obstacle, and scrapes bottom
5 U-boat illuminated by car headlights

to Kirkwall

St. Mary's

Loch of Ayre

HOLM
(part of Orkney Mainland)

Kirk Sound

Howequoy Head

Skaildaquoy Point

SCAPA FLOW

Lamb Holm

Skerry Sound

Glims Holm

Weddell Sound

Burray

Holm Sound

Rose Ness

St. Nicholas Church

Cornquoy (farm)

Path of *U-47*
Blockship

2000m
1600
1200
800
400
0
1 nautical mile
.8
.6
.4
.2
0

Orkney
Kirkwall
Mainland
Scapa Flow
Hoy
South Ronaldsay

Kirk Sound as it looks today, viewed from Cotland, Holm. The line of the No. 1 Churchill Barrier is clearly visible, leading from the mainland to the island of Lamb Holm. In October 1939 the line of blockships lay just beyond where the barrier now crosses the channel. The hills in the distance are on the island of Hoy, at the far side of Scapa Flow. The main fleet anchorage was approximately where the oil tanker can be seen riding at her moorings, off the low-lying island of Flotta. (Courtesy of Reg Jamieson, RN [rtd])

west, which was intended to take them into Kirk Sound. They held the course for five minutes, and could see the loom of the land on either side of them. Then the water beneath them began to drop away rapidly, until the sounder indicated less than 3m under the boat's keel. Spahr suddenly realized his mistake – they were entering Skerry Sound, not Kirk Sound. On the bridge they noticed there was only one blockship – not three. Prien turned the boat hard to starboard, and steered a course of 030 degrees until they regained sight of the Orkney mainland, a few hundred metres to the west of the little church. This time Spahr gave a fresh course of 260 degrees, and they turned to port, to enter Kirk Sound. Any further doubt vanished when the outline of a blockship appeared in front of them, lying parallel to the shore. It was *Numidian* – the first and least effective guardian of the channel.

It was now well after midnight, and the window of slack water had passed. They could feel the growing strength of the tide pushing them as they worked their way past *Numidian*, leaving her on their starboard side. Prien later described her as a two-masted schooner. The value of the Luftwaffe reconnaissance photograph was now clear – it gave Prien a useful bird's-eye image of the channel ahead of him, and the obstacles that lay in his path. They were barely 150m from the northern shore of the sound, but there was no sign of life. Prien knew that 1,000m to the west lay the little fishing village of Holm village – officially called St Mary's. The chances of passing it without being seen must have seemed slim. Then they spotted the main line of blockships.

Ahead of them – at right angles to their course – lay the remains of *Soriano*, while to the south of her – off the boat's port bow – lay the third blockship, *Thames*. Prien had thought about this during the voyage – whether it was best to attempt to pass between the two blockships, or to pass close under the bow of *Soriano*, or even *Thames*. The current seemed stronger there as it pressed against the hulls of the blockships, picking them out with a line of white water. Prien noticed it do the same for a pair of anchor cables, which effectively blocked the gap between the two wrecks.

OPPOSITE

Penetrating Scapa Flow's defences: *U-47* in Kirk Sound, 14 October 1939.

GB 16800 bc
Nur für den Dienstgebrauch
Bild Nr. 224/40/066 (Lfl. 5)
Aufnahme vom 8. 10. 40

Lamb-Holm (Scapa Flow)
Befestigungsanlagen

Länge (westl. Greenw.): 2° 54′ 42″ Nördl. Breite: 58° 53′ 12″
Mißweisung: — 14° 04′ (Mitte 1940) Zielhöhe über NN 15 m

Maßstab etwa 1 : 13 200

Genst. 5. Abt.   Januar
Karte 1 : 100 000
GB/Sc Bl. 4

In this Luftwaffe reconnaissance photograph of Kirk Sound taken in the summer of 1940 the three blockships in the channel have been augmented by others. Ignoring *Numidian* to the right, the others, from top (north) to bottom are *Gambmira* (which later drifted into *Numidian*), *Soriano*, *Redstone*, *Thames* and *Neuchatel*. The shore of Lamb Holm can be seen in the bottom right of the picture. This effectively blocked the channel until No. 1 Churchill Barrier was built.

So, he made the split-second decision to pass to the north of *Soriano*. It was a fortunate decision – the gap between the two blockships was also spanned by a thick hawser, with anchor chains suspended from it. If the boat had become entangled there the mission would have ended in disaster.

The boat was turned slightly to port, a movement exaggerated by the current as it pressed on the stern of the turning boat, pushing it even further to the side. Then, ahead of him, Prien saw another plume of white water, marking where an anchor cable entered the water. It was the line which ran from the bow of *Soriano* to the northern shore of Kirk Sound. The steel cable sloped down from the bow of the blockship at an angle of 45 degrees. If the boat was snagged on it then she would be pinned there by the tide, unable to work herself free. If she went to starboard of it she could run aground. Exactly what happened next is unclear, as subsequent accounts vary.

Prien's log stated simply, 'I pass the two-masted schooner [*Numidian*], which is lying on a bearing of 315 degrees, plenty of room, with 15m to spare. In the next minute the boat is turned by the current to starboard. At the same time I recognise the cable of the northern blockship [*Soriano*] at an angle of 45 degrees ahead. Port engine stopped, starboard engine slow ahead, and rudder hard to port, the boat slowly touches bottom. The stern still touches the cable, the boat becomes free, it is pulled round to port, and brought back on to course again with difficult rapid manoeuvring.'

This suggests that Prien passed the obstacle to port, so that the spot where the cable entered the water was on the starboard side of the boat. In other words he sailed as close as he could under the bows of *Soriano*, and hoped the cable would pass safely over the conning tower of the boat. Even with the periscopes retracted this would have given him a clearance of just a metre or so. This sounds almost suicidal. It is more likely that he turned the boat to starboard, then spun her to port using the technique he described. This means that the reference to the U-boat 'touching bottom' refers to the keel scraping its way along the seabed as it passed. The boat then edged away to port, but the port quarter – the port side of the boat's stern – still touched the cable as it did so. Then the boat surged past the obstacle and freed itself of the obstacle.

Whatever took place, Prien was fortunate that his boat hadn't become snagged or run aground. If the cable entered the water halfway between the bows of *Soriano* and the shore, then it would have been approximately 80m from the shore. Even at high water Prien had barely enough space to squeeze past the obstacle and the shallows. A clear indication of just how hazardous this was is the fact that when he passed back through Kirk Sound after the raid, he did so at the southern end of the channel, well away from *Soriano* and her troublesome anchor cable. However, for the moment that particular obstacle lay behind them. Ahead of them lay deeper water, and then Scapa Flow. To starboard lay the little fishing village of St Mary's, while beyond it was the small headland of Skaildaquoy Point. It was at that moment that a light shone from the shore, catching the conning tower of the U-boat in its beam.

The beam came from the headlights of a car – a taxi. Earlier that evening garage owner Bobby Tullock from Kirkwall was asked to drive a group of passengers – Gordon Highlanders – to the Holm Hall, in St Mary's. His 1930s Dagenham-built Ford V8 was used as a taxi – a rarity in wartime Orkney, and so Mr Tullock set off for Holm. The soldiers were from O Company, which was stationed in Holm, and it transpired that they had been drinking in Kirkwall and were absent without leave. They forced Mr Tullock to secrecy, threatening him with dire consequences if he reported them. It was with some relief that he dropped them off by the hall, where a dance was being held. The hall was set back a little from the main road, which ran between the houses and the shore. As he reached the main road Mr Tullock paused for a minute or so, to regain his composure. While he was there, his one headlight shone across Kirk Sound.

If he had looked up, Bobby Tullock might have spotted Günther Prien, passing just a few hundred metres in front of him. However, due to wartime regulations the taxi only had one working headlight, on the driver's side, and it was taped up so only a thin rectangle of light shone from it. In these conditions it was hard enough to see the road in front of the car, let alone spot passing U-boats. So, Mr Tullock put the Ford into gear and turned right onto the main road. A further 250 yards up the road he made a sharp turn to the right, and then continued on towards Kirkwall, six miles to the north.

U-47 in Kirk Sound (overleaf)

Kapitänleutnant Prien's choice of Kirk Sound as his route into Scapa Flow was based on a Luftwaffe reconnaissance photograph, and possibly on the evidence supplied by German intelligence gathered between the two wars. The photograph showed only three blockships in place, of which one – SS *Numidian* – had been pushed out of line during the inter-war years; instead she lay parallel to the shore. She was no longer an obstacle to Prien. That left the American freighter SS *Soriano*, scuttled in March 1939, and the old steamship RMS *Thames*, scuttled in 1915. Between the two lay a tangle of cables, designed to obstruct the centre of the channel. Prien decided to pass close by *Numidian*, and then cut under the bows of *Soriano*, between the blockship and the northern shore of the channel. As he drew close Prien spotted the anchor cable of the freighter in front of him. He tried to swerve around it to starboard, passing so close inshore that the bow of the boat briefly scraped the bottom of the channel. The stern of *U-47* then snagged against the cable, before a combination of the boat's engines and the current wrested her free. Having passed the line of blockships, Prien found himself inside Scapa Flow.

Kirkwall garage owner Bobby Tullock (second from left), pictured beside the British-built Ford Model 48 V8 car he was using as a taxi on the night of 13–14 October 1939. Due to wartime regulations, only one headlight would have been working and its beam was reduced to a narrow rectangle of light. (Collection of the Tullock family, Kirkwall)

When the tail lights of the taxi disappeared around the corner, the bridge crew of *U-47* were unsure whether they had been spotted, and the car driver was planning to raise the alarm. At any rate there was nothing they could do about it.

Prien had the intelligence information supplied by aerial reconnaissance which showed him what could be seen from the air, but it didn't reveal the presence of hidden dangers such as minefields, submerged obstacles or nets. It was only when the U-boat passed Skaildaquoy Point without incident, and the depth sounder reported deeper water beneath the keel, that Prien realized they had breached the defences, and were now in Scapa Flow. They had done it! He spoke into the intercom, and passed the news to the rest of the crew: 'We are in.' Now, all they had to do was to find a suitable target, torpedo it, and escape again without being caught.

The attack

Now that *U-47* was safely inside Scapa Flow, Prien began searching for prey. The large natural harbour was a little over 8 nautical miles long and 6 wide, and visibility was limited – probably no more than 4,000 to 5,000 yards, or 2 to 2.5 nautical miles. In all likelihood it was less – possibly as low as between 3,000 and 3,500 yards. However, the Luftwaffe's recent aerial photographs gave him some idea of where to look. Just as it had been in the last war, the main anchorage for capital ships lay to the south-west, just north of the island of Flotta. While this was almost 5 nautical miles away, Prien and his bridge crew would be able to spot the ships well to the east of Flotta. He could then decide what ship to target and how to attack her. Behind this main anchorage lay the small islands of Cava, Fara and Rysa Little.

The aerial photographs had shown that this was where the auxiliary warships anchored, along with store ships, hospital ships and other non-combatant vessels. The only warship of note here was the old dreadnought *Iron Duke*, which now served as a floating headquarters. Beyond Cava was the destroyer anchorage, although other destroyers could well be scattered elsewhere inside Scapa Flow. Further to the west was Bring Deeps, where the boom marked the start of Hoy Sound. To the south – somewhere off the U-boat's port beam – was the boom at Hoxa Sound, which ran between the eastern tip of Flotta and Hoxa Head, the most westerly part of South Ronaldsay. Both of these areas were to be avoided, as

Prien expected them to be patrolled, and for boom vessels to be operating there. He would be spotted and the alarm raised before he could carry out an attack on a more prestigious target.

Off the boat's starboard beam was the northern arm of Scapa Flow, which extended for almost 5 nautical miles, as far as Scapa Bay, and Scapa Pier. While warships were sometimes anchored in this area, Prien felt the best hunting ground was the main anchorage off Flotta. *U-47* had just rounded Skaildaquoy Point, and to starboard lay Howequoy Head, a small headland that marked the point where the coast fell away to the north, towards Scapa Bay. Apart from the headland no other land could be seen. The order was given and the boat altered course slightly to port, onto a new heading of 250 degrees – approximately west-south-west. The speed of the boat had been reduced to around 10 knots. Gradually they saw the low hill that marked the western end of Burray appear to port, as well as the small island of Hunda that lay off its western tip.

This study of *Kapitänleutnant* Günther Prien was produced by the Kriegsmarine as a colour postcard and sold as a souvenir in Germany after the raid on Scapa Flow. Other crew members were also sketched for posterity by naval artists.

Beyond Hunda the anchorage opened out to the south, towards Hoxa Sound and the boom defences. That meant that Flotta was somewhere ahead of them. Prien estimated that on their present course they would arrive off the northern edge of the main fleet anchorage in approximately 15 minutes. By then he would be able to see what ships were lying there, and plan his attack. The looming mass of Hoxa Head could be seen to the south, and with it came the risk of being spotted by a patrol boat. The bridge crew claimed to have spotted one – or else a boom defence boat – lying to the west of the headland. Fortunately for them, though, the chances of being spotted were slim, unless lookouts were scouring the anchorage behind them. That, though, was unlikely. Then the coast of Flotta appeared, off the port bow. Prien and his men would have stared intently through their binoculars, straining for a glimpse of the dark hull of a warship set against the lighter black around it. Instead they saw nothing.

They were now almost halfway between Howequoy Head and the main anchorage, but still no ships were spotted. Surely a capital ship would have appeared in sight by now? Reluctantly, Prien and his men began to think that the anchorage was empty. In fact, several warships were at anchor there. The modern light cruiser *Belfast* lay at anchor off the main jetty on Flotta's north coast, while the older light cruiser *Caledon* was anchored 1,000 yards to the east of her. A little to the north-west, between Cava and Fara, were the equally old light cruisers *Cardiff*, *Colombo* and *Delhi*. While all of these were legitimate targets, particularly *Belfast*, none of them were capital ships – battleships, battlecruisers or aircraft carriers. They were what Prien was searching for, and looking for in vain. However, due to the blackness of the night, and the black backdrop of the small islands, Prien and his men were unable to spot the cruisers.

As *U-47's* First Watch Officer, *Oberleutnant zur See* Engelbert Endraass (1911–41) was Prien's second-in-command, and was on the bridge of the U-boat during the attack on *Royal Oak*. He went on to command his own boat, *U-567*, but was killed when she was sunk in December 1941.

When they saw the hump-backed shape of Cava, with nothing obvious lying in front of it, they concluded that the main anchorage was deserted. By now the north-east tip of Flotta lay approximately 4,800m to the south-west, while Cava, at the far end of the main anchorage, was 8,700m due west of them, off the boat's starboard bow. Between the two lay Fara, 9,600m away. Prien later described the scene in his war diary: 'It is disgustingly light. The whole bay is lit up. To the south of Cava there is nothing. I go further in. To port I recognise the Hoxa Sound coastguard, to which in the next few minutes the boat must present itself as a target. In that event all would be lost; at present south of Cava no ships are to be seen, although visibility is extremely good.' The claim that the night was a light one is not borne out by other observers, who claim the opposite – it was a dark night, with relatively poor visibility.

In any case, in his charting of the raid, the U-boat's navigator Obersteuermann noted this spot on the chart as marking the deepest penetration of the U-boat into Scapa Flow. That meant they were closer to the shore of Holm than they were to Flotta. Despite what Prien claimed in his diary, the chances of being spotted were slim. If he failed to see the outline of light cruisers some 5,000m ahead of him, it was unlikely a patrol boat in Hoxa Sound could detect the low shape of a U-boat at the same distance. Similarly, it is surprising Prien could see a patrol boat at that distance, on a largely moonless night. Still, it was approximately 12.42am on the morning of 14 October, and Prien had no target. The longer he remained in Scapa Flow, the greater the chance of being detected. So, having seen no warships in the main anchorage, Prien ordered the boat to turn around and head back towards Howequoy Head. In truth, if the U-boat had continued on its original course Prien would have spotted the *Caledon*.

Within minutes they had completed the slow turn and were heading back towards the coast of Holm. Instead of maintaining a reciprocal course towards Howequoy Head, Prien then angled the boat slightly further towards the north, on a heading of approximately 050 degrees. The U-boat was making around 8 knots, so it took them around six minutes to regain sight of the coastline of Holm, which would have appeared as a black line set against the dark night sky. From what happened next, we can assume that visibility at this stage of the operation was now less than 4,000m. In all likelihood it was just over 3,200m. The coast would have come into view at around 12.52pm, but Prien held the course for a few more minutes, to work his way closer inshore. He then turned the boat to port, so that she was running parallel to the coast, approximately 1,000m from the shore. By keeping the black outline of the land on his starboard side, Prien had a visual reference to help him as he headed towards Scapa Bay.

According to the U-boat's navigator, *U-47* maintained this course for another five minutes, covering a distance of approximately 1,200m. Then, Prien and the bridge staff saw something looming out of the darkness ahead of them. It was the unmistakeable outline of a battleship. She lay approximately 3,000m ahead of the U-boat and 1,000m to the west of the low cliffs lining the eastern shore of Scapa Flow. She lay at anchor, with her bows pointing towards the shore, so the bridge crew of *U-47* saw her from her starboard side. At that angle she lay almost beam on, although not quite, as the battleship was actually facing east-south-east. Prien stopped the boat, and as she glided to a standstill he ordered the forward torpedo tubes to be prepared for firing.

U-47 had four bow tubes – two on either side of her centreline. Of these, tubes 1 and 3 on the port side and tube 2 on the starboard side were already loaded with Type G7e electric torpedoes. Tube 4 on the starboard side carried a G7a torpedo, which was powered by compressed air. Prien wanted to use the electric torpedoes, as they didn't produce a wake, and therefore they wouldn't betray the U-boat's firing position. So, he decided to engage the target with three of his four torpedoes. The G7e T2 (Type 2) torpedo was first developed during the 1920s as part of a secret Reichsmarine programme. The disadvantage of these wakeless torpedoes was their relatively limited range and speed through the water – 5,000m and 30 knots respectively. This, though, wasn't a problem for Prien, as the target was well within range, and she was also at anchor, meaning that torpedo speed was irrelevant.

In fact, it was almost a perfect textbook firing position. At that range – approximately 3,000m – a torpedo travelling at 30 knots, or 926m per minute, would take just over three minutes to reach its target. In the forward torpedo room of *U-47 Obermechanikersmat* (Petty Officer) Kurt Bleek made the necessary adjustments to the torpedo settings, following the instructions relayed to him from the Torpedo Data Computer (TDC). On the bridge, *Obergefreiter* (Leading Seaman) Rudolf Smyczek had already entered in the target's approximate range and bearing, and noted that she wasn't moving. The TDC was an electromagnetic analogue computer which added to this the U-boat's course and speed, and the parameters of the torpedo. The machine made the necessary trigonometric calculations and produced the torpedo settings needed to hit the target.

With these calculations complete, everything was ready. The whole process would have taken less than a minute to complete. Prien then gave the order to fire. Endrass manned the attack periscope, whose cross-hairs had provided the TDC with the bearing information it needed. The aiming point was just beneath her forward superstructure. At 1.02am, three torpedoes were launched from *U-47*, one after the other. All three launched without any problems, and as soon as they did the torpedo tubes were closed and drained, in case the tubes needed to be reloaded again. This involved draining the water into compensation tanks, together with enough extra water volume to compensate for the weight of the torpedoes. The aim was to avoid any sudden changes to the boat's trim when the torpedoes were fired. Then they waited.

1.02AM, 14 OCTOBER

U-47 fires three torpedoes at apparent target of two battleships

1.05AM, 14 OCTOBER

One torpedo explodes at the bow of *Royal Oak*

The scene on board the drifter *Daisy II* on the morning of 13 October as she ferried libertymen (off-duty sailors) from *Royal Oak* on to Scapa Pier. From there the men would spend the day in Kirkwall. Within 24 hours many of these sailors would be dead.

U-boat veterans have said that the seconds that tick by during a torpedo run seem to pass with agonizing slowness. On the bridge, *Oberleutnant* Amelung von Varendorff had pressed the button on a stopwatch when the first torpedo was launched. So did Spahr the navigator. He watched the seconds tick by. Everyone kept staring at the target – or targets. In his war diary, Prien wrote, 'Two battleships are lying there at anchor, and further inshore, destroyers. Cruisers not visible, therefore attack on the big fellows. Distance apart, 3,000 metres. Estimated depth 7.5 metres. Impact firing.' There is little doubt Prien and his bridge crew thought they saw two battleships at anchor ahead of them, even though there was only one. Similarly, the sighting of destroyers lying inshore beneath the cliffs of Gaitnip is incorrect, as all the destroyers in Scapa Flow at the time were lying at anchor off Lyness, 9 nautical miles away to the south-west.

That night, the only target Prien could see was *Royal Oak*. The darkness of the moonless night and the loom of the land to starboard were playing tricks on the U-boat crew. The only other naval vessel anywhere ahead of them was the old seaplane carrier *Pegasus*, anchored halfway between *Royal Oak* and Scapa Pier, approximately 6 cables (or 0.6 nautical miles, 1,200 yards or 1,097m) to the north of the battleship. As *Pegasus* displaced

7,080 tons, and was 366ft (112m) long, she would probably have been completely obscured by the battleship, which had a displacement of 29,970 tons, and was 620ft (189m) long. If *Pegasus* was visible at all – highly unlikely at a range of more than 4,000m – only her foredeck would have been visible from Prien's vantage point, the rest of the ship being obscured by *Royal Oak*. In all probability the U-boat crew saw nothing beyond the battleship, unless they imagined it.

First impact

Some 3,000m to the north, aboard the battleship *Royal Oak*, most of the crew were asleep. Shortly after 1.05am one of *U-47*'s three torpedoes struck the starboard bow of the battleship. While one witness on *Royal Oak* recorded the time as being a minute earlier, the later time was noted by both the crew of the U-boat and the bridge watch of *Pegasus*, both of whom were using accurate marine chronometers rather than watches. The torpedo's 300kg (126lb) charge detonated with a sharp explosion and sent a cascade of water high into the air. The whole battleship seemed to shake – towards the stern, in the officers' cabins, it felt as if a giant terrier had picked up the battleship and shaken her. Strangely this sensation was felt more towards the stern than near the bow, where the explosion actually took place. There, though, the effects were far more dramatic.

Sailors were thrown out of their hammocks by the explosion, and an acrid smell of smoke drifted through the compartments. On the bridge, Leading Signalman William Fossey noted the time – 1.04am by the bridge clock – and while he missed the cascade of water he saw an anchor cable run out. The two main bow anchor cables of *Royal Oak* ran up through the hawsepipes on the port and starboard side of the bow, and across the foredeck to the capstans – one for each cable. From there they dropped down through naval pipes to their respective cable lockers. Another cable on the starboard side of the forecastle served the smaller sheet anchor. The three capstans were locked, and a cable stopper – a screw slip – was rigged just forward of each of them, to prevent the cable slipping accidentally. Some accounts say both bow cables ran out – others claim just the starboard one went. In fact, it was just the starboard cable that ran out when its screw slip had broken, and the cable had soon stopped paying out as it was also secured below decks in the cable locker.

The Officer of the Watch – Lieutenant Michael Benton RM – called over to John Gatt, skipper of the drifter *Daisy II*, which was tethered to the battleship's port side. Gatt had no idea what caused the bang, but assured the officer that it hadn't come from his drifter. By then Captain William Benn had arrived on the foredeck, accompanied by his First Lieutenant, Commander Reg Nichols. The two officers were joined by others and began taking charge. They asked if anyone had heard an aircraft – no one had. The possibility of an air attack wasn't completely dismissed, though, but no bomb damage was reported. Instead, reports came in that there was minor flooding in some of the stores near the bows. It began to look more like an accidental explosion than anything else. After all, the battleship wasn't

THE ATTACK ON HMS *ROYAL OAK*

1AM–1.45AM, SATURDAY 14 OCTOBER 1939

Shortly after 1am on 14 October, the German U-boat *U-47* commanded by *Kapitänleutnant* Prien launched a surface attack on the battleship HMS *Royal Oak*, as she lay at anchor inside Scapa Flow. The range was a little over 3,000m, so it took three minutes for the spread of three torpedoes to reach their target. Only one of them hit, striking the battleship on her starboard bow. On board the battleship the resulting detonation was thought to be the result of an internal explosion, and the damage control teams reacted accordingly. Most of her crew returned to their hammocks, leaving the duty watch to deal with the situation.

Ten minutes later a second salvo of three torpedoes was fired, and at 1.15am two of these struck the starboard side of the battleship. The second of these torpedo hits caused a secondary explosion which produced a fireball that swept through the lower decks of the ship. The battleship immediately began to list heavily to starboard. Within five minutes *Royal Oak* had capsized. Then at 1.29am she finally sank, leaving a pitifully small number of survivors in the oil-covered water. Many of these men were rescued by the battleship's tender, the drifter *Daisy II*, but 833 crewmen lost their lives during the attack. Her job done, *U-47* escaped from Scapa Flow without incident.

KEY

HMS *Royal Oak* – Royal Sovereign class battleship

HMS *Pegasus* – seaplane carrier

U-47 – Type VIIb U-boat

■ EVENTS

1. 1.02am – *U-47* fires a spread of three torpedoes at her target.

2. 1.05am – One of these three torpedoes strikes the battleship, on her starboard bow. The alarm is raised, and damage control parties gather on the foredeck.

3. 1.05am – Explosion seen and heard from HMS *Pegasus*, and noted in the ship's log.

4. 1.06am – Prien turns *U-47* to starboard, and fires a single torpedo from her stern tube at the target, which misses.

5. 1.09am – Having reloaded three of her bow tubes, *U-47* turns again and heads towards her target.

6. 1.10am – A boat is launched by *Pegasus* and ordered to investigate the cause of the explosion.

7. 1.12am – *U-47* fires a second spread of three torpedoes at *Royal Oak*, from her second firing position.

8. 1.15am – Two torpedoes strike *Royal Oak* amidships, approximately 15 seconds apart.

The battleship immediately begins to list heavily to starboard.

9. 1.16am – Prien turns *U-47* around and heads at high speed towards Kirk Sound, the channel he plans to use to escape from Scapa Flow.

10. 1.17am – The drifter *Daisy II* breaks free from the port side of *Royal Oak* and commences picking up survivors.

11. 1.20am – *Royal Oak* capsizes. Men are still standing on her upturned hull.

12. 1.29am – *Royal Oak* finally sinks.

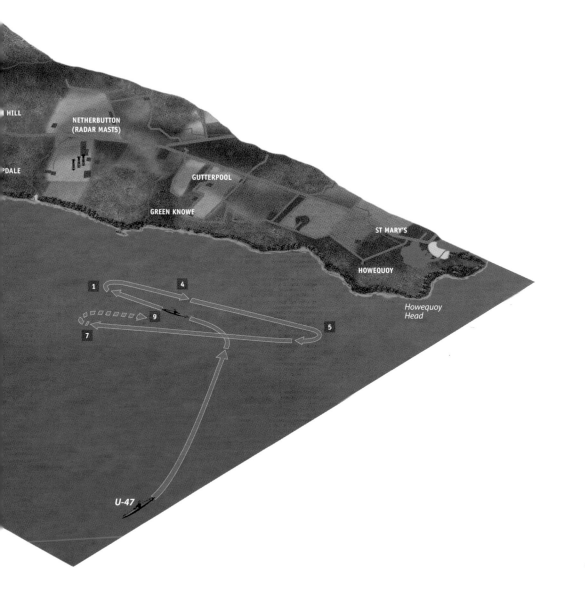

Sailors gather beneath the forward 15in gun turrets of HMS *Royal Oak*, in a picture taken before the outbreak of war. The starboard anchor cable in the foreground was cast loose when the first torpedo struck the starboard bow of the battleship, just behind the photographer's viewpoint, and it ran out for several seconds before it was halted by a securing shackle inside the cable locker.

sinking and there was no sign of external damage. The possibility of a torpedo hit wasn't even considered.

Gradually, a semblance of order was restored. Hundreds of men had emerged on deck, after either being pitched out of their bunks or from concern about the explosion. It was felt these men would get in the way of the duty watch, who were trying to deal with the situation. So, they were ordered to return to their messdecks. As a precaution, a pipe (announcement) was made over the tannoy, 'Away launch crew' and 'Take magazine temperatures'. Both were understandable precautions. If there had been an internal explosion then it was important to check that there wasn't a risk of a fire somewhere near the forward magazines. So, Lieutenant John Moore led an inspection party forward to read the magazine temperatures. Neither he nor his men survived what followed.

The launch crew were called out to carry out an external inspection of the ship – the launch was a much more useful vessel for this than the larger steam pinnace, which was already secured alongside. However, there is no evidence that the launch had been lowered before events overtook the operation. On the *Daisy II*, Skipper Gatt was also requested to raise steam and stand by for further orders. Rear Admiral Henry Blagrove appeared on deck, wanting to know what had taken place, but after being assured everything was under control he returned to his cabin, at the stern of the battleship. The operation of the ship wasn't his responsibility, so he rightly left matters in the hands of Captain Benn. In the battleship's Sick Bay, the duty medical team treated any crew who had suffered minor injuries when they were thrown from their hammocks.

Meanwhile, Commander Nichols tried to find out exactly what had happened. One of his first orders – as a precaution – was to release the two men held in the ship's brig (prison), which was located beneath the forecastle. Then reports began to reach him, helping him narrow down the source of the explosion. By now two theories had developed. The first was that there had been an explosion among the bottled CO_2 cylinders, which were kept in a store forward, and used to power the ship's refrigeration system. The compartment was checked, and both the machinery and the cylinders were undamaged. A more likely candidate was either an inflammable liquid store or a boatswain's store in the bows, below the waterline, where the bang had been heard. A damage control team was sent below to investigate. Like Lieutenant Moore's party, none of these men returned alive.

Meanwhile, Skipper Gatt noticed something floating in the water. He told *Royal Oak*'s Officer of the Watch, who ordered Signalman Fossey to switch on an Aldis signalling lamp. There was something there, and Fossey was ordered to abandon the Aldis in favour of a searchlight. It was used to illuminate the water off the battleship's port side, in front of the *Daisy II*. Floating in the water were pieces of wood and a mass of straw. Nobody knew it at the time, but this was wreckage which had been blown out of the starboard side of *Royal Oak* following the torpedo hit. Back on board, most of the men who had appeared on the upper deck had drifted back to their messdecks. Some, though, remained cautious, and loitered a little, to find out what had happened. That hesitancy probably saved their lives.

Others heard the explosion too. On board *Pegasus* the duty watch could barely see the battleship – only her outline was visible – but they heard the explosion. One stoker recalled that it sounded like a giant hammer being hit against their own ship. The ship's log recorded the event: '01:05 Explosion in Royal Oak'. Nobody could see anything untoward, but the officer of the watch decided to send one of the seaplane tender's own motor boats over to the battleship to investigate. Five minutes after the explosion the boat was in the water and on her way. On the west side of Scapa Bay at the small farm of Foveran – now a restaurant – farmer John Laughton heard the bang and went outside to investigate. While he saw *Pegasus* clearly enough, *Royal Oak* was just over 3,900 yards (3,500m) away and invisible in the darkness. He went back to bed.

On the other side of Scapa Bay, in the small farm of Borrowstonehill, teenager Harry Russell recalls being woken by a loud bang. He and his father thought it was a horse kicking the door of the adjacent stable, so they got up to investigate. The horses were asleep, so Harry and his father had no idea what had caused the noise. They never

This view of the inside of the control room of a Type VII U-boat shows just how cramped conditions were on board. Just behind the helmsman's seat in the foreground are the periscope and the ladder leading to the conning tower.

imagined it came from the battleship, 3,500 yards away to the south-south-east, and out of sight behind the hill at Gaitnip. On board *Royal Oak* the minutes ticked by, but still neither Captain Benn nor Commander Nichols had discovered the cause of the explosion, although the Chief Shipwright reported the ship was flooding, probably in the paint store. That wasn't particularly serious, as the compartment was already sealed off, and it was forward of the battleship's watertight collision bulkhead which lay just in front of the anchor hawsepipes. It had now been over ten minutes since the explosion, and both Nichols and Benn were convinced the explosion had been an internal one.

In fact, one of *U-47*'s three T2 torpedoes had struck the battleship approximately 10ft below the waterline, and 2ft aft of the bow. It had ripped a hole in the side, a gash that was more vertical than horizontal. There were five compartments right in the bows of the ship. The uppermost one was the seamen's forward heads (toilets) on the main deck, where the damage control party reported burst pipes and smashed urinals. Below this on the lower deck was a paint store, which sat on the waterline of the ship. Below this was the platform deck, where the compartment housed an inflammable liquid store. Below that again on the hold deck was an empty watertight compartment, which sat just above the ship's keel plates. The vertical hole in the battleship's starboard side ran through three of these compartments, from the paint store on the lower deck to the empty compartment on the hold deck.

All these three unoccupied compartments had filled with water, but they were so small the flooding hadn't altered the trim of the battleship. Instead *Royal Oak* continued to ride peacefully at anchor. Some 3,000 yards away to the south, Prien and his bridge crew had been waiting for their spread of three torpedoes to hit the battleship. Two of them missed, but at least one had hit its target, resulting in what might have seemed like a satisfying column of water. Then – amazingly – nothing else seemed to happen. There was no sign of alarm on the battleship. Prien and his men had expected the anchorage to spring to life, for searchlights to seek them out and for destroyers to give chase. Instead, the battleship remained peaceably at anchor. *Oberleutnant* Endrass later commented that it was almost as if they were taking part in a peacetime exercise.

Prien decided it was safe to reload two of the three empty bow torpedo tubes and to make another attempt at sinking the battleship with a spread of three torpedoes – one being the G7a torpedo in tube 4. It would take about ten minutes to carry out the task. He ordered the U-boat to turn to starboard, and as *Ober-Mechanikersgefreiter* (Leading Mechanic) Kurt Bleeck and his torpedomen began moving two spare T2 torpedoes into the tubes, *U-47* crept southwards again at slow speed. Before the battleship slipped from view, though, and as the TDC still had a firing solution registered, Prien decided to fire his stern torpedo. In the U-boat's after torpedo room two leading seamen flooded the tube and acknowledged the tube was ready. The torpedo was launched at approximately 1.08am, shortly before the boat turned to starboard again, and headed back towards the battleship. The torpedo missed its target.

OPPOSITE

The forward torpedo room of a Type VII U-boat – a space that also doubled as the crew's mess, hence the folded bunks visible behind the torpedomen. They shared this cramped space with 12 torpedoes, one of which is being primed here, ready for use.

By now the reloading of the forward tubes was almost complete and the calculations made by the TDC were updated. Thanks to the turn when the battleship appeared again in the darkness, they were approximately 700m to the west of their original firing position. Prien had been convinced he had seen two battleships at anchor when he launched his first attack. He even wrote in his log, 'One torpedo fired at the northern ship, two at the southern. After a good 3½ minutes a torpedo detonates on the northern ship. Of the other two nothing is seen.' This time, though, *Royal Oak* was almost exactly at right angles to the path of the torpedoes. Prien would be making a textbook attack and this time he concentrated on the battleship he could clearly see, rather than imagined targets behind her. At 1.12pm *U-47* fired a second spread of three torpedoes. Once again the seconds were counted off on the bridge stopwatch, as the torpedoes sped towards their target.

The fatal hits

At 1.15am, two torpedoes struck the starboard side of HMS *Royal Oak*. The third torpedo missed. To maintain buoyancy on a U-boat torpedoes are fired one after the other, several seconds apart. That is exactly how they arrived at their target. The first torpedo struck the battleship amidships, well below the waterline. A huge column of water was thrown up, followed by an explosion, the flame of which reportedly reached the top of the battleship's mainmast. Approximately 15 seconds later a second torpedo struck the ship, hitting her slightly further aft. This triggered a third explosion, caused by the combustion of ammunition. Any one of these explosions would probably have inflicted a mortal blow on the old battleship. The combination of the three in quick succession meant that *Royal Oak* sank in 13 minutes, taking almost two-thirds of her crew down with her.

The two torpedoes hit the battleship amidships, an area which in theory was well protected, forming part of the battleship's armoured citadel. However, the armoured belt of Royal Sovereign-class battleships only extended 5ft below the waterline when the ships were fully laden. As the draught of *Royal Oak* was just over 30ft (probably a little more as her oil tanks were 90 per cent full) this meant that the lower portion of her hull was unprotected by the armoured belt. This was because the belt was designed to protect the battleship from enemy shells rather than torpedoes. The main protection of the battleship below the waterline consisted of an anti-torpedo bulge and a transverse torpedo bulkhead. The bulkhead lay inside the outer hull of the ship – the sandwich-like space between these two protective barriers was used to hold fuel oil. Where the torpedoes struck this torpedo bulkhead was 1.5in (3.75cm) thick. Behind it lay another sandwich – a 2in (5cm) air gap between the bulkhead and the engine room bulkhead behind it.

This degree of underwater protection was barely sufficient to protect the battleship against German torpedoes when she entered service in May 1916. It was much less so in 1939, given inter-war improvements in torpedo design. It was widely acknowledged that the Royal Sovereign class was poorly protected against torpedo attacks – much less so than its predecessors of the Queen Elizabeth class. So, in the 1920s anti-torpedo bulges were fitted

to these battleships – *Royal Oak* received hers in 1922–24. This protective layer formed a bulge or blister which extended beyond the outer hull and ran the whole length of the armoured citadel – almost the entire ship apart from the forecastle and quarterdeck. Its name derived from its shape – it bulged out from the sides of the ship, and reached its widest point three-quarters of the way between the waterline and the keel. The bulge then curved back to join the outer hull a little above the point where the hull curved inwards towards the ship's keel.

The anti-torpedo bulge created a curved protective barrier, beyond the outer hull of the ship. The idea was that a torpedo would strike this and detonate, blowing a hole in it rather than in the outer hull of the ship, or even the torpedo bulkhead behind it. Effectively, it was a sacrificial shield. The space inside the bulge was divided into three lateral sections, so that a hit against one wouldn't flood the whole cavity inside the bulge. In other ships of her class this cavity was filled by crushable steel tubes, designed to absorb some of the impact of the blast. These weren't fitted in *Royal Oak*, so only an air space lay between the blister and the outer hull. The first torpedo from the salvo to hit the ship pierced the anti-torpedo bulge with ease and detonated against the outer hull behind it. The torpedo warhead blasted a large hole in the steel outer hull and in the torpedo bulkhead that lay beyond it. The explosion sent up the column of water reported by observers and water began pouring into No. 1 Boiler Room.

Above the battleship's engine spaces on her starboard side were two levels of messdecks. The engineers' messdecks on the lower deck were directly above the point of impact, while above them on the main deck was the messdeck used by the boy seamen. As a capital ship relegated to second

The remains of a German Type 2 G7e electric torpedo were discovered on the seabed of Scapa Flow, close to the wreck of *Royal Oak*. Subsequent research has revealed that the torpedo was issued to *U-47* in October 1939. The surviving torpedo mechanism is now on display in the Stromness Museum, Orkney.

A reconstruction of the wreck of *Royal Oak*, as she lies 16 fathoms (96ft, or 29.3m) below the surface of Scapa Flow. She rests on her starboard side superstructure, while amidships on her starboard hull she still bears the holes from two torpedo hits. In this view the damage inflicted to her bow by the first torpedo hit is visible as a vertical tear below what was once the battleship's waterline.

1.15AM, 14 OCTOBER

Two more torpedoes hit *Royal Oak*, causing a massive secondary explosion

line duties *Royal Oak* had a large proportion of boy seamen on board – youngsters under the age of 18. Between the two decks was a 2in-thick layer of hardened steel, which formed the uppermost surface of the armoured citadel. Above that again was another 1¼in-thick armoured deck, dividing the lower deck from the upper (or battery) deck. There were only six places where hatchways pierced these decks, so access from one deck to the other was restricted. Once on the battery deck men could reach the quarterdeck towards the stern of the ship, or climb another level to reach the forecastle deck. The armour designed to protect the innards of the ship was almost as effective at keeping trapped men from escaping.

When the first of these two torpedoes struck, most of the crew were in their hammocks on their respective messdecks, either sleeping or trying to get back to sleep after the earlier explosion. The whole ship shuddered under the impact, and steel bulkheads and metal fittings shook violently. Many of the men were thrown from their hammocks, or if they were berthed amidships they were killed in the explosion. Elsewhere dazed men and boys realized the ship had been hit, and began untangling themselves from their hammocks and heading towards the compartment doors or ladders that led out of their messdecks. Approximately 15 seconds later the next torpedo struck the ship and punched a hole in the torpedo bulkhead in front of the main engine room. This time no column of spray was seen – instead there was a thick column of smoke, caused by atomized fuel from the starboard tanks which had just been ripped open. The battleship immediately began to heel over to starboard.

Then came the third explosion in less than a minute. To some, it merged with the previous explosion, while others heard two distinct detonations. The likelihood is that the second explosion of the sequence detonated cordite charges in a magazine serving the starboard battery of 6in guns. Rather than exploding immediately, this detonation created a fireball which swept through the central portion of the ship. This was the real killer blow. The magazine was below the Marines' messdeck, and the fire swept through the space, before reaching the open air through the battery deck. Hundreds of men were burned alive by the blast, many of them still in their hammocks. Others had been clambering up ladders leading onto an upper deck, only to suffer the same fate, as the fireball roared through the decks and hatchways.

Some of the men who were crowding to escape through doors or hatches were knocked to the ground by the second explosion, as the deck seemed to heave beneath them. Most were still picking themselves up when they were caught by the fireball. Sergeant George Booth RM remembered seeing men with their flesh hanging off them. There also seems to have been more than one wave of flame. Leading Stoker Thomas Jones was clambering up a ladder onto the battery deck when the man ahead of him was caught by the fireball. He fell down, and a second ball swept over him as he lay there. Survivors said of the oncoming wall of flame, 'It was like looking into the muzzle of a blowlamp – the flame was bright orange outside, and an intense blue inside.' Some men tried to dodge out of the way of the fireball, and some survivors remember that it seemed to seek them out. For others there was no escape.

The flooding of the engine room also closed down the ship's electrical circuits, and at the same time as the fireball swept through the lower deck and main deck the battleship was plunged into darkness. The last two explosions had ripped internal compartments away, and men became trapped by the wreckage. The ship was already listing about 15 degrees to starboard, but following this last explosion the battleship suddenly lurched even further over. Below decks, the only illumination was the burning of hammocks and mess tables, or flames from bodies whose clothing was still on fire. Water was pouring into the ship now, and as the vessel heeled over objects began to come loose and slide across the deck, while men – both alive and dead – slid with them. There was by then no doubt that *Royal Oak* was sinking – the list had now increased to around 45 degrees. If the crew were to survive, they had to reach the upper deck.

The problem was that there were only six hatchways leading through the armoured citadel onto the main deck, and a similar number leading up from there. A crush of men gathered around the ladders beneath these hatchways, while behind or below them they could hear the screaming of their dying or horrifically injured shipmates. It is understandable that a sense of panic was gripping many of the men, particularly those with more than one hatch to climb through to reach the upper deck. Senior rates urged the men to steady themselves, but in many places it had become, as one survivor put it, 'a case of survival of the fittest'. In some places doors or hatches had been wedged shut by the list of the ship, and men tried in vain to force their way through them. In some cases they gave up, and ran to the side of the ship, to open the starboard portholes and escape that way. In port the regular glass portholes had been replaced by wooden ventilators. These had to be removed before anyone could squeeze themselves through the small circular opening. For many it was impossibly tight.

John Gatt, master of the 100-ton drifter *Daisy II*, which served as *Royal Oak's* tender while she lay in Scapa Flow. Although a civilian, Gatt, a fishing skipper from Rosehearty in Aberdeenshire, was awarded a naval honour – the Distinguished Service Cross (DSC) – for saving the lives of 386 crew of *Royal Oak*.

The portholes were as much a danger as a means of escape. While regular portholes were watertight, the ventilators were not. Eventually, when the battleship heeled over far enough, those on the starboard side would start letting in water and that would speed up the sinking. On the port side, men saw sky above them as they struggled through the ports and onto the outer hull. On the starboard side the heeling of the ship meant that anyone escaping that way would be caught as the ship rolled onto her side. The hatchways through the armoured decks were equally deadly. Each of them was fitted with a steel hatch cover mounted on rollers. These were designed to be slid over the hatches when the ship went into action, to reduce the risk of plunging shells finding their way through the hatches into the armoured citadel.

As *Royal Oak* heeled over many of these hatchways slid shut. Sergeant Booth was climbing a ladder when the armoured hatch rolled shut above him, cutting the two men ahead of him in half.

Water was now rising through the lower deck, and those who were too slow or injured to escape, or who had become disoriented or trapped, were doomed. On the main deck above them, men were still fighting to escape. Those who remained calm fared better than others – below one hatch, Corporal James McLaverty RM – a veteran of the previous war – was a voice of hope helping the younger men through to safety before he joined them. Once through the hatches, the men found a way onto the upper deck. Some simply went to the casemates for the 6in guns and stepped through them, while others worked themselves forward or aft, depending on where they were. One by one they emerged on the upper deck, where at least they had a chance of saving themselves.

Men who jumped off the starboard side risked being crushed as the ship rolled on top of them. Those on the port side had to clamber down the outside of the hull before they reached the water. The *Daisy II* had been alongside the port side of *Royal Oak* when she was torpedoed, and before she could work free the drifter was caught by the heeling of the ship. The anti-torpedo bulge rose beneath her, catching the bows of the small boat and lifting them clear of the water. The drifter's engines tried to pull her astern, but all they did was churn up the water where men were jumping off the starboard side of the quarterdeck. Skipper Gatt shut off his engines and hoped for the best. Finally she broke free, her bows crashed into the water, and her crew began the task of rescuing oil-covered men from the water.

Over on the starboard side some men had clambered into the ship's pinnace, which had been tethered alongside. Over a hundred men found refuge there, but the boat overturned owing to their weight. The Admiral's gig had also been thrown clear of the quarterdeck, and although she was floating upside down she acted as a makeshift liferaft. Commander Nichols and other men had freed a few Carley floats – the heavy old-fashioned liferafts carried by the battleship – and had thrown them in the water. Many of them had been smashed during the storm off Fair Isle a few days before, but anything that floated would help save lives. Church service benches were hurled over the side, too, and in the water men clung to them as they tried to swim free of the ship before she turned over. As more men came on deck they found it harder to reach the water than the men ahead of them.

The hull was now heeling so much that the starboard anti-torpedo bulge was almost clear of the water. Within seconds the ship would be on her side. Some men recalled clambering down the hull as far as the bilge keel – the protruding ledge at the base of the bulge – before throwing themselves into the oil-covered water. Others slid down, cutting themselves badly on barnacles as they did so. Men in the water began singing, to attract the attention of Skipper Gatt. He conned his drifter through the clumps of men, then he and his crew hauled people on board the overcrowded boat. Finally – at around 1.20am the *Royal Oak* rolled over. Men in the water remember seeing some of their shipmates still standing on her hull as she sank.

Survivors recall hearing the sound of moving pieces of machinery tumbling as she rolled, and saw men being thrown into the water. Then her underside lay there for a few minutes, settling very slowly. A searchlight from *Pegasus* suddenly illuminated the scene, revealing men still standing on her upturned hull, unsure what to do next. A few jumped into the water – others didn't. Then, at 1.29am, *Royal Oak* slipped from view. After the violence of the last 14 minutes some men watching from the water might have expected a more dramatic end. Instead she went quietly. It was 16 fathoms to the seabed – 96ft (29.3m), where the battleship came to rest – a tomb for the hundreds of men and boys still inside her. She landed on her starboard side, but rolled over to port, crushing her funnel and masts under her own weight until she rested on the starboard side of her superstructure, with her keel pointing towards the surface. That meant the underside of her hull was just 17ft (5.2m) below the surface of Scapa Flow. There *Royal Oak* remains, a war grave, undisturbed by divers save an annual Royal Naval inspection team, who fly a white ensign over her as a sign of respect.

After *Royal Oak* sank, the *Daisy II* continued to pick up survivors, until she was so overloaded she had to leave the scene and take the men to *Pegasus*. The seaplane carrier had launched her boats, too, and these also began rescuing people. Other men swam towards the cliffs lining the shore at Gaitnip, 1,000m away to the east. Many survivors recalled seeing men overcome by their injuries and sinking beneath the water, or simply giving up the struggle against the cold water and the clinging oil. Men were heard singing to keep up their spirits – *Daisy Daisy, Give me your answer do* being

The sinking of *Royal Oak* (overleaf)

When the first torpedo hit HMS *Royal Oak* at 1.05am it was assumed the explosion was an internal one – nobody in authority thought the battleship was under attack. There was no room for doubt ten minutes later, when *Royal Oak* was hit again. Two torpedoes struck her starboard side and inflicted mortal damage on the old ship. The first struck her amidships and ripped a hole in her hull around her boiler rooms. Approximately 15 seconds later the second torpedo struck her a little further aft and the explosion blew a hole in the side of her engine room. This second blast caused a secondary explosion – the detonation of a magazine – and a fireball tore through the lower decks of the ship, incinerating anyone in its path. The battleship began to heel over after the first midships hit, and after the second explosion this list became even more pronounced. There was no doubt that *Royal Oak* was capsizing, and anyone left below decks would go down with her. As the ship heeled over, crewmen struggled through hatches and even portholes to reach the upper deck. There they jumped into the oil-covered water, or walked down her increasingly exposed hull to step off the ship. Within ten minutes of being hit *Royal Oak* had capsized – a few minutes later she plunged beneath the waters of Scapa Flow, taking 833 of her crew down with her.

The forward control tower of *Royal Oak* once sat at the top of the foremast, and served as a gunnery director for the battleship's main guns. It now lies beside the ship, as the foremast was bent over and crushed by the weight of the hull as the ship rolled over.

a popular one, as the drifter made her rounds of the survivors. Petty Officer Richard Kerr recalled, 'It seemed I was alone on a wide, open sea.' He tried swimming to the cliffs, but gave up and swam towards a light in the distance. It turned out to be the anchor light of *Pegasus*, which he reached after what seemed like hours in the water, but was probably less. Survival time in the water of Scapa Flow in October is less than an hour.

After being rescued the survivors were brought aboard *Pegasus*, where their wounds were tended, they were cleaned up and put in a hammock or bunk. Cigarettes, cocoa and hot rum were in plentiful supply, as were blankets. One man, though, had a more important mission to perform. When he came on board, Captain Benn made his way to the bridge and ordered a signal to be sent to Admiral French – the Admiral Commanding Orkney and Shetland, reporting that *Royal Oak* had been sunk by enemy torpedoes. He also requested boats to help search for survivors. At 2am, the news was passed on to the Admiralty in London – '*Royal Oak* sunk in Scapa Flow – Series of explosions'. Then a little after 5am a second signal passed on the cause of the sinking: 'Report from Captain Benn. He believes *Royal Oak* was torpedoed.' Even then the Admiralty queried the news, seeking confirmation it wasn't due to an air attack. By 3am the first of three destroyers were ordered to start the search for an enemy U-boat. By then, though, Prien and his men were already on their way home.

The escape

On the bridge of *U-47*, Prien and his bridge crew had watched and waited as their spread of three torpedoes headed towards the battleship. Prien's war diary described what they saw: 'After three tense minutes comes the detonations on the nearer ship. Then comes columns of water, followed by columns of fire and splinters through the air.' It is interesting that Prien still believed he saw two battleships anchored in front of him, rather than just one. From that angle *Pegasus* would have been completely hidden, and even if she could have been seen at that distance she was hard to mistake – she looked more like a freighter than a battleship. Prien later went on to name the second capital ship as the battlecruiser *Repulse*, even though she was over 200 miles to the south at the time, safely ensconced in the dry dock at Rosyth.

Having watched two of his three torpedoes hit the starboard side of the battleship, Prien ordered the U-boat to start her engines and turn to starboard. He expected the hunt for him to begin immediately and so every minute counted. He later justified his withdrawal, claiming that his tubes were empty, he couldn't remain on the surface without being spotted and that he couldn't attack at night while he was submerged. He even repeated his claim that there were destroyers anchored between *Royal Oak* and the shore. So, the U-boat turned southwards again and ran at full speed – almost 18 knots – towards Howequoy Head and the entrance to Kirk Sound.

Prien's war diary also claimed that at that moment 'The harbour springs to life. Destroyers are lit up, signalling starts on every side, and on land 200 metres away from me cars roar along the roads'. This was pure invention. There were no destroyers and the only ship to send any signals was *Pegasus*, relaying the news of the disaster to the Hoxa Head communication centre, 8 nautical miles to the south. The Kirkwall-Holm road was actually 2,000m away, and for the most part it was hidden by the small hump of Howequoy Hill. Any drivers who were on the road would have been oblivious to what was going on in Scapa Flow. The only other lights or boats Prien saw would have been further south – the patrol vessels guarding the Hoxa Boom. Otherwise the anchorage remained strangely silent.

The confusion in the diary continued. It claimed it was now low tide and the current was against the boat as it entered Kirk Sound. The tide was ebbing, but it was far from low tide, and the U-boat was actually helped along by the current. Rather than risk the shallows to the north of *Soriano*, Prien decided to take the southern side of the channel, passing as close as he could under the bows of the blockship *Thames*. Prien cut his speed to 10 knots until he gauged the size of the gap in front of him, and then increased speed before reaching the line of blockships. The diary records, 'At high [speed] I pass the southern blockship [*Thames*] with nothing to spare. The helmsman does magnificently. High speed ahead both, finally three-quarter speed, and [then] full ahead all out.' They shot past the line of blockships and almost hit what Prien described as a 'mole' – probably the rocks off the northern side of Lamb Holm, where the Churchill Barriers now run. The U-boat swerved hard to port to avoid them and then resumed its course.

This wreck buoy marks the site of the wreck of HMS *Royal Oak*. As a designated war grave she is 'off limits' to unauthorized divers. The buoy bears the inscription, 'This marks the wreck of HMS *Royal Oak*, and her crew. Respect their Resting Place.'

**1.29AM,
14 OCTOBER**

The capsized *Royal Oak* sinks in 96ft of water

Once safely past the eastern end of Lamb Holm, Prien turned the head of the boat towards the south-west and the open sea. They were out. That meant they had spent barely two hours in Scapa Flow, although it must have seemed much longer. As the survivors from *Royal Oak* were being helped from *Daisy II* to *Pegasus*, the men who had sunk their ship were safely outside Scapa Flow and stealing away from Orkney under cover of darkness. It would be another 45 minutes before the first destroyer would arrive off the western end of Kirk Sound to begin its search for a U-boat. According to some of her crew, Prien's announcement that they had sunk one battleship and damaged another was met by a chorus of cheers, and a case of beer was produced to help celebrate their triumph. Best of all, they were all alive to tell the tale.

At dawn on the morning of Saturday 14 October *U-47* was 35 nautical miles north-east of the fishing port of Fraserburgh, north of Aberdeen. Prien claims to have seen a glow from Scapa Flow before he submerged for the night, but that was impossible – the anchorage was 80 nautical miles behind him. Just as she had during her outward voyage, *U-47* spent the day lying submerged on the seabed, 100m below the surface of the North Sea. At 7.35pm the boat surfaced again, pausing as usual at periscope depth so Prien could sweep the horizon with his periscope, to make sure they were alone. He still had torpedoes left – one in the stern tube and four in the bow. There was always a chance they might come upon a merchant ship during the night, and Prien wanted to be ready.

Just before 9pm someone turned on the radio and tuned in to the BBC. There the crew of *U-47* learned the name of their victim. The BBC announcer reported, 'The Secretary of the Admiralty regrets to announce that HMS *Royal Oak* has been sunk, it is believed, by U-boat action.' It was confirmed – they had sunk a battleship. Prien later expressed regret that there was no mention of his imagined second ship. However, by the time the U-boat returned to Germany the news had swept around the world.

The boat got under way again and Prien noted that visibility was reasonably good, except towards the Scottish coast out of sight to the west. Until then, Prien had followed his outward bound course, but that night he decided to head due south, towards the mouth of the Firth of Forth. The reason was to increase his chances of encountering a merchantman. It also meant they avoided the allotted patrol area of another U-boat, *U-20*, commanded by *Kapitänleutnant* Möhle. In fact *U-20* was already on her way back to Kiel. By 6am *U-47* had reached a point 72 nautical miles due east of St Andrews, on the coast of Fife. Once again the boat submerged during daylight, this time lying at a depth of 72m. At 10am they heard the sound of depth charges going off in the distance – either an attack on another suspected U-boat or an exercise. Prien and his men remained where they were and slept as best they could.

11.44AM, 17 OCTOBER

_U-47_ moors at Wilhelmshaven to a triumphant welcome

Kapitänleutnant Günther Prien being congratulated by Admiral Hermann Boehm following the safe arrival of *U-47* in Wilhelmshaven shortly before noon on 17 October. Hundreds of naval and civilian well-wishers were there to welcome home 'The Bull of Scapa Flow'. On this occasion Boehm was accompanied by both *Grossadmiral* Erich Raeder and *Kommodore* Karl Dönitz.

On 20 October a skeleton crew sailed *U-47* from Wilhelmshaven to Kiel by way of the Kaiser Wilhelm Canal. Prien and the rest of the crew joined her in time to make a triumphal entry into the naval port. In this photograph, *U-47*, bearing her new 'Bull of Scapa Flow' emblem, is cheered by the crew of the light cruiser KMS *Emden*.

At 6.23pm on the evening of 15 October Prien took the boat back to periscope depth with more caution than usual. They had already heard the sound of a vessel – possibly a merchant ship – and Prien sought her out using his periscope. It was a merchant ship. She turned out to be the 3,162-ton Bergen Line passenger ship SS *Meteor*, en route from Bergen to Newcastle. As a neutral vessel Prien should have left her well alone, but then the U-boat's wireless operator reported that she was sending a signal. Prien ordered the boat's bow gun to be manned and fired a warning shot. In fact, the German telegraphist was mistaken – the *Meteor* hadn't been signalling at all. Prien apologized and let the vessel continue on her way. Once she was out of sight Prien swung the boat round onto a south-westerly course and continued at full speed.

Shortly before dawn on the morning of 16 October they had almost crossed the shallow waters of the Dogger Bank when they spotted three mines drifting close to the boat. Prien continued gingerly, and at 7.02am he submerged for the day. When he surfaced just before 7pm the sea was empty of either boats or rogue mines. So, they continued on their heading of 128 degrees, until they reached Channel 1 – the entrance to the German Defensive

Minefield. By 4am the following morning they were through the channel, and shortly afterwards they sighted the islands fringing the German coast. That morning, *Oberleutnant* Endrass and a party of volunteers set about decorating the U-boat. In white they painted a symbol of a snorting, charging bull on either side of the conning tower – 'The Bull of Scapa Flow'. In the process, Prien acquired a new nickname.

Rather than returning to Kiel, Prien headed to Wilhelmshaven, and at 11am they came within sight of the port. By 11.44am *U-47* tied up alongside the quay. Nine days before their departure from Kiel had been a quiet one, reflecting the covert nature of their mission. On their return they found the port lined with cheering well-wishers, bands playing and admirals waiting to greet them. At their head was *Kommodore* Dönitz, the man who had masterminded the raid. On Tuesday 17 October *Kapitänleutnant* Prien and his men found themselves fêted as

The snorting bull emblem drawn by *Oberleutnant* Endrass and others on both sides of *U-47*'s conning tower on the morning of 17 October was designed the previous day by the boat's navigator, *Obersteuermann* Spahr. It later became the logo used by the entire 7th U-boat flotilla.

heroes, and about to be flown to Kiel and Berlin, where they would parade through the streets and Prien would be taken to meet Adolf Hitler.

Meanwhile, 500 nautical miles away in Scapa Flow, the base was under attack again. On the morning of 17 October four German Ju 88 bombers appeared over the anchorage, but the only large target they could find was *Iron Duke*, moored close to the Naval Hospital Ship HMS *Abba*, where the wounded survivors from *Royal Oak* were being treated. All of their bombs missed the old battleship, but one landed so close alongside that its blast damaged her hull and *Iron Duke* began taking on water. The old battleship was beached, and remained so for the rest of the war. Two days before, on the morning of 15 October, the wounded had been transferred from *Pegasus* to a hospital tender, and then on to *Abba*. *Pegasus* then steamed south to the main anchorage, where the survivors were transferred onto the transport ship *Voltaire*. Meanwhile, smaller launches combed the rocks beneath the cliffs off Gaitnip, rescuing a few survivors from the shore, but finding many more bodies washed up on the rocks.

Throughout the day the landward approaches to the shore had been sealed off by the army, as the bodies and survivors were removed. By late afternoon they had gone and the young Harry Russell walked down from Borrowstone to the shore behind Gaitnip. There he found the body of a young sailor lying in a rocky cove. The teenager ran to Scapa Pier to report the discovery. Strangely, this incident didn't stop him from joining the Royal Navy when he was old enough – he would later return to Scapa on board a battleship. On the west side of Scapa Bay a young girl – now Naismi Flett – went beachcombing with her friends, and was delighted to find kitbags and caps on the beach. She was too young to realize why they were there. Over in Lyness, as Prien was being introduced to Hitler, a Board of Enquiry was being held, which – it was hoped – would reveal why so many young men had died that night, and how a U-boat had managed to penetrate the defences of Scapa Flow.

ANALYSIS

While Günther Prien's raid on Scapa Flow was highly successful, it could be argued that its impact on the effectiveness of the Home Fleet was minimal. After all, *Royal Oak* was no longer a front-line battleship – she could no longer keep up with the rest of the fleet. If Prien had penetrated Scapa Flow's defences a week earlier, the far more important battleships *Nelson* and *Rodney* were in the anchorage, accompanied by the battlecruisers *Hood* and *Repulse,* and the aircraft carrier *Furious.* The sinking of any of these ships would have dealt a serious blow to the Royal Navy. *Nelson* was the flagship of the Home Fleet, while *Hood* was probably the Royal Navy's best-known capital ship. To minimize the importance of *Royal Oak* is not to denigrate the memory of the men who served and were lost in her. It merely accepts the fact that by 1939, the ageing *Royal Oak* was nearing the end of her days as a useful member of the British fleet.

German achievements

The success of the raid should thus be considered less for what it achieved – the sinking of *Royal Oak* – than for the propaganda value the raid had in Germany, and around the world. *U-47* and her crew had achieved what had proved impossible during the previous war. Three German U-boats had tried and failed to penetrate Scapa Flow's defences, and two of them had been sunk. *U-47* had not only succeeded, but it had sunk a battleship. This was an achievement worth celebrating. Like Prien and his men, the staff on board *Kommodore* Dönitz's headquarters ship first heard of the attack when it was announced by the BBC. However, they caught an earlier broadcast than Prien, made on the morning of 14 October.

The news spread. On the day after Prien's safe return, the headline of the German newspaper *Der Angriff* declared, 'Terrible Blow for England – *Royal Oak* and Repulse torpedoed in Bay of Scapa Flow'. The addition of *Repulse* came from an interview with Prien, who stood by his original story. Subsequent versions of the tale became even more inventive, culminating in

Kapitänleutnant Günther Prien and U-47's engineering officer *Oberleutnant* Hans Wessels pictured being driven through the streets of Berlin on 18 October, on their way to the Reich Chancellery, and Prien's meeting with Adolf Hitler. Thousands of Berliners lined the route to cheer the officers as they passed.

a ghostwritten account of the raid called *Mein Weg Nach Scapa Flow* ('My Journey to Scapa Flow') written on Prien's behalf by journalist Paul Weymar. Published in 1940, the book was a bestseller in Germany and was subsequently reprinted in English. Prien's account was heavily embellished. Events were added that didn't take place, such as the pursuit of the U-boat by destroyers, or those that did happen were over-dramatized, such as the sinking of *Royal Oak*, which Weymar described as being torn apart by the explosion. This was all unnecessary – the achievement of Prien and his crew was considerable enough without it needing to be embellished by the German propaganda machine.

On 17 October Prien and many of his men were flown to Kiel and then to Berlin in Hitler's own plane the following morning. Cheering crowds lined the route from Tempelhof Airport to the Reich Chancellery. There Prien was introduced to Hitler, who wanted to know the details of the raid. Then, Hitler presented Prien with the Knight's Cross of the Iron Cross. Now Prien was not only a war hero – he was a highly decorated one. The rest of the crew were awarded lesser versions of the Iron Cross. The round of celebrations continued for some time, but by 16 November both Prien and his U-boat resumed their duties, and left on their third patrol of the war. These patrols would continue until 7 March 1941, when *U-47* – with Prien in command – was sunk with all hands to the south of Iceland, during an attack on Convoy OB-293.

Kommodore Dönitz was also a beneficiary of the successful operation. He was promoted to the rank of *Konteradmiral* ('Rear Admiral'), a promotion backdated to 1 October, and named *Befehlshaber der Unterseeboote* ('Supreme Commander of U-boats'). After the raid on Scapa Flow, U-boats represented the future of the Kriegsmarine, and Dönitz would oversee a dramatic expansion of their role. The fact that the sinking of

In Germany the round of ceremonies, speeches and congratulations continued for several days. In this photograph, taken on 24 October, Prien (centre) and Wessels (left) are congratulated by representatives of the Krupp Germaniawerft shipyard in Kiel, where *U-47* was built. It was not until 16 November that Prien and his crew resumed active duties and the boat sailed on her third war patrol.

Royal Oak did little to alter the fighting potential of the Home Fleet was never mentioned. For Germans the real success of the mission was the Kriegsmarine's proven ability to strike at the very heart of British naval power and to avenge the naval humiliations of the previous war.

British failures

The Board of Enquiry into the sinking of *Royal Oak* was held on Wednesday 18 October. As *Iron Duke* was damaged, the board met in a store shed at nearby Lyness. The Board's job was to determine whether *Royal Oak* had been torpedoed by a U-boat, and if so, then how had the boat entered

Kapitänleutnant Günther Prien, pictured receiving the *Ritterkreuz des Eisernen Kreuzes* (Knights Cross of the Iron Cross) from the Führer of Germany Adolf Hitler, in a ceremony held in the Reich Chancellery on 18 October – the day after Prien and his crew returned to port. Hitler demanded that Prien give him a full account of the raid during a celebratory luncheon held after the presentation.

Scapa Flow. It was also charged with looking at how the battleship had sunk. Finally – and most importantly – the Board was to determine what needed to be done to prevent such an attack happening again. It took six days to hear the evidence and make its deliberations. In the end there was little doubt that a U-boat had managed to enter Scapa Flow and had carried out the attack. The way the U-boat got in and out of the anchorage was less easy to determine, but a case was made for Kirk Sound, although as Admiral French put it, this would involve a considerable feat of seamanship. He told the Board, 'Kirk Sound is definitely not impregnable, although extremely difficult due to the strength of the tide.'

As the evidence was gathered, the weaknesses of Scapa Flow's defences were laid bare. There were gaps in the blockships covering the eastern entrances. The booms at Hoxa Sound and Hoy Sound were insubstantial and poorly protected. No searchlights or gun batteries covered the eastern channels, while the other main channels were still poorly defended. It was concluded that none of the entrances into Scapa Flow were truly impregnable. In Kirk Sound – the most likely entrance used by the U-boat – the only defences, apart from a pair of rusting blockships, were tide and current. The Board's report put this to the Admiralty as diplomatically as it could: 'We are left with the impression that the problem of blocking the eastern sounds before the war was not handled as adequately as its importance deserved.' It went on to blame delays in improving the defences on the Admiralty, saying that the blockships ACOS planned to have put in place would have been there were it not for delays imposed by the Admiralty.

So, far from the Board of Enquiry being a cover-up – as some historians have claimed – it was the very opposite. It blamed the Admiralty for not putting adequate defences in place earlier, for starving ACOS of resources and for placing the fleet at risk through its lack of commitment to rendering Scapa Flow secure. The Board exonerated Captain Benn of *Royal Oak* of any blame, but exposed just how ineffectual the battleship's defences had been against torpedoes. The anti-torpedo bulges had proved completely useless, as had the torpedo bulkhead. The findings made grim reading for the crews of the nine remaining British battleships of a similar vintage.

Within days the blockships ordered by ACOS were used to seal off the eastern entrances into Scapa Flow. Soon gun batteries would appear covering Holm Sound and Weddell Sound. Minefields, induction loops and extra

A commemoration ceremony is held over the wreck of *Royal Oak* on 18 October every year. In 2014, the 75th anniversary of the sinking, the short but poignant wreath-laying ceremony was held on board HMS *Bangor*, with two other vessels in consort. These annual commemorations ensure that the 833 dead of HMS *Royal Oak* are remembered by Orcadians and naval personnel alike.

anti-submarine nets would protect the two main entrances, just as they had done during the previous war. The newly created inter-services committee, formed to protect Scapa Flow, went even further. It approved the construction of new airfields, dramatically increased the size of Scapa's anti-aircraft defences, and the latest radar equipment was installed to protect the anchorage even further. By the time the Home Fleet returned to Scapa in May 1940 the anchorage was on its way to becoming the best defended harbour in Europe. There would be no repeat of the *Royal Oak* debacle.

Still, conspiracy theories continued to circulate. It was claimed that a German watchmaker based in Kirkwall was responsible for sabotaging the *Royal Oak*; no such German national existed. Others have claimed that the old battleship *Iron Duke* was also hit, even though she was at the far end of Scapa Flow at the time of the attack. Similarly the second battleship Prien claimed to have seen was variously reported as being *Repulse*, *Renown* and *Hood*. Admiralty ship movement reports prove none of these ships were present. Some British newspapers and servicemen even doubted a U-boat could be responsible for the disaster, claiming the *Royal Oak* was sunk by sabotage – either through a bomb planted by the clockmaker, or by a deliberately triggered internal explosion. The wreck itself proves the lie to these notions. Rather, the *Royal Oak* and her crew fell victim to a daring attack, and a rare feat of courage and seamanship. The Admiralty realized this – hence the steps to prevent such an attack happening again.

The final measure – and one that benefits Orkney to this day – was the construction of four barriers across the eastern channels – work carried out by a combination of civilian contractors and Italian prisoners-of-war. To avoid the complaint that the Italians were being used to aid the British war effort, the building of the 'Churchill Barriers' was deemed a civil construction project to improve communications, as a road was placed over the top of them. That road was opened in May 1945 – four days after the end of the war with Germany – and it is still being used today. The barriers and the road are, perhaps, the only lasting legacies of Prien's raid on Scapa Flow. Another beneficial short-term legacy was the changing of the Admiralty's rules on Boy Seamen. The British press were horrified that so many youngsters had died on *Royal Oak*. So Boy Seamen were removed from ships on active service, and kept out of harm's way – at least until they came of age.

All this did little to comfort the relatives of the 833 men and boys of *Royal Oak* who lost their lives that night. For them the news of the sinking was followed by days of waiting for news. The newspapers were quicker to report the scale of the losses than the Admiralty, but for many the lack of official word offered a glimmer of hope. For many, that was snuffed out when the casualty lists were published and the official telegrams were sent out. Even the survivors were scarred by their experience – both physically and mentally. A high proportion of them suffered varying degrees of burn damage, and many never fully recovered from their injuries. Just 26 bodies were recovered and were buried in the Naval Cemetery at Lyness. For the remainder, the only marker over their resting place is the green wreck buoy in Scapa Flow that marks the site of the great steel war grave lying beneath it. Every year, in a quiet and dignified ceremony, the dead of *Royal Oak* are remembered, and wreathes cast into the water over the site. For the crew of *U-47*, no such tributes can be offered, for they are lost forever in the vastness of the North Atlantic. For them, their only headstone is the sea itself.

OPPOSITE
After her attack on Scapa Flow *U-47* conducted eight more war patrols, between November 1939 and March 1941, when the U-boat was lost with all hands. From the summer of 1940 on she was based in the French port of Lorient. This photograph shows *U-47* returning to Lorient at the end of her eighth patrol, in late October 1940.

CONCLUSION

While *Kapitänleutnant* Günther Prien and his men carried out the raid on Scapa Flow with considerable skill and daring, this enterprise – codenamed 'Special Operation P' – was the brainchild of *Kommodore* Karl Dönitz, the Kriegsmarine's *Führer der Unterseeboote* (Commander, U-boats). For him, the raid was as much about eradicating the shame of defeat from the previous war as striking a serious blow against the Royal Navy's Home Fleet. In Germany, Scapa Flow had assumed a near-legendary status as a naval fortress. By penetrating its defences Dönitz's selected boat and crew would expunge this shame, while demonstrating the long reach and fighting prowess of the Kriegsmarine's U-boat arm. In this the raid was a complete success.

While *Royal Oak* was not a front-line warship, she was still a powerful battleship, and therefore a prestigious target. She was also the only capital ship in Scapa Flow when *U-47* breached the defences of the anchorage, and so she became Prien's victim. With hindsight, it is easy to say that more could have been done to prevent such a heavy loss of life. However, this was not the finding of the Board of Enquiry, who agreed that *Royal Oak*'s officers and men had reacted appropriately to the first hit, as it seemed inconceivable that the resulting damage was caused by an enemy torpedo. When the next two torpedoes struck the battleship, the damage caused was so extensive that her crew were powerless to save their ship, and for that matter most of their shipmates.

Setting aside the high human cost of the attack, Prien's raid on Scapa Flow can be seen as an extremely bold undertaking, particularly as the crew thought their chances of survival were no better than their predecessors had been during the previous war. The passage through Kirk Sound called for the highest level of seamanship and professionalism, as did the less dramatic but equally daring exit through the same channel. This is why the raid ranks highly in the annals of naval history, and is rightly regarded as one of the most significant submarine operations of World War II.

FURTHER READING

Numerous documents were consulted for this book, including ships' logs, official reports, personal accounts and enquiry statements, housed either in the National Archives, the National Maritime Museum or the Deutsches Marinemuseum ('German Naval Museum'). For a more general bibliography, all the books listed below are either still in print or available from good libraries. Some are of dubious value, having been based largely on Prien's dramatized ghostwritten account. However, Sarkar, McKee and Weaver are particularly valuable for their emphasis on the testament of *Royal Oak* survivors.

Attwood, E. L., *Warships: A Text Book on the Construction, Protection, Stability, and Turning of War Vessels* (London, Longman, 1911)

Brown, Malcolm and Meehan, Patricia, *Scapa Flow: The Reminiscences of Men and Women Who Served in Scapa Flow in the Two World Wars* (London, Allen Lane Ltd, 1969)

Burt, R. A., *British Battleships of World War One* (Barnsley, Seaforth Publishing, 2012)

Frank, Wolfgang, *Enemy Submarine: The Story of Günther Prien, Captain of U-47* (London, William Kimber Ltd, 1968)

Friedman, Norman, *Battleship Design and Development, 1905–1945* (New York, NY, Smithmark Publishing, 1979)

Kurganov, Alexander, *The Phantom of Scapa Flow: The Daring Exploit of the U-47* (Shepperton, Ian Allen Ltd, 1974)

Parkes, Oscar, *British Battleships, 1860–1950* (London, Seeley, Service and Co., Sons, 1973)

Prien, Günther, *U-Boat Commander* (London, Allan Wingate Ltd and Howard Baker Ltd, 1969)

Prien, Günther, *Mein Weg nach Scapa Flow* (Berlin, Im Deutschen Verlag, 1940 – published in English as *I Sank the Royal Oak* (London, Gray's Inn Press, 1954)

McKee, Alexander, *Black Saturday: The Royal Oak Tragedy in Scapa Flow* (Bristol, Cerberus Publishing, 2004 – first published by London, Souvenir Press, 1959)

Sarkar, Dilip, *The Sinking of HMS Royal Oak: In the Words of the Survivors* (Stroud, Amberley Publishing, 2012)

Snyder, Gerald S., *The Royal Oak Disaster* (London, William Kimber and Co., 1976)

Turner, David, *Last Dawn: The Royal Oak Tragedy at Scapa Flow* (Glendaruel, Argyll Publishing, 2008 – first published as *Ultimate Sacrifice* by Ely, Melrose Press, Ely 2004)

Weaver, H. J., *Nightmare at Scapa Flow: The Truth about the Sinking of HMS* Royal Oak (Edinburgh, Birlinn, 2008 – first published by Colwall, Cressrelles Publishing, 1980)

INDEX

References to illustrations are shown in **bold**